Self-Evident

Self-Evident

DISCOVERING THE IDEAS AND EVENTS
THAT MADE THE DECLARATION OF
INDEPENDENCE POSSIBLE

TIM PATRICK

Copyright © 2017 by Tim Patrick
Published by Owani Press in Seattle, Washington

All rights reserved. No part of this book may be used or reproduced in any manner whatsoever without written permission, except in the case of brief quotations in critical articles and reviews.

For more information on this book, contact the author, Tim Patrick:

    Website: wellreadman.com
    Email: tim@timaki.com
    Facebook: facebook.com/wellreadman
    Twitter: twitter.com/thewellreadman
    Goodreads: goodreads.com/wellreadman

The Peace-loving Crocodile logo and "Understand in One Afternoon" are trademarks of Owani Press. Visit Owani Press online at OwaniPress.com.

Printed by CreateSpace, an Amazon.com company.

Publisher's Cataloging-in-Publication Data
    Names: Patrick, Tim--1966-, author
    Title: Self evident : discovering the ideas and events that made the Declaration of Independence possible / Tim Patrick.
    Series: Understand in One Afternoon
    Description: Includes index and bibliographical references. | Seattle, WA: Owani Press, 2017.
    Identifiers: ISBN 978-0-9964654-3-4 | LCCN 2017917335
    Subjects: LCSH United States. Declaration of Independence. | United States. Declaration of Independence--Signers. | United States. Declaration of Independence--Criticism, Textual. | Jefferson, Thomas, 1743-1826--Books and reading. | Jefferson, Thomas, 1743-1826--Social and political views. | United States. Continental Congress, 1776. | Enlightenment--Great Britain--Colonies. | Enlightenment--United States. | BISAC HISTORY / United States / Revolutionary Period (1775-1800) | POLITICAL SCIENCE / American Government / General
    Classification: LCC E221 .P38 2017 | DDC 973.3--dc23

ISBN-13: 978-0-9964654-3-4 (paperback)

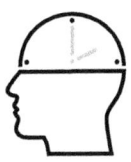

CONTENTS

INTRODUCTION... XI

CHAPTER 1: ORIGIN AND PREAMBLE..................... 1
    ORIGIN OF AUTHORITY 2
    DOCUMENT DATE... 4
    DOCUMENT TITLE 20
    PREAMBLE 21
    UNALIENABLE RIGHTS 25

CHAPTER 2: DECLARATION OF NATURAL RIGHTS..... 25
    PURPOSE OF GOVERNMENTS................................ 30
    FAILURE OF GOVERNMENT 32
    PATIENCE AND DUTY OF THE GOVERNED.................. 34
    APPLICATION TO THE COLONIES 36

CHAPTER 3: LIST OF GRIEVANCES 41
    KING GEORGE III, THE TYRANT 43
    NOTICE TO A CANDID WORLD 45
    GRIEVANCE 1 47
    GRIEVANCE 2 48
    GRIEVANCE 3 50
    GRIEVANCE 4 52
    GRIEVANCE 5 53

- Grievance 6 56
- Grievance 7 58
- Grievance 8 60
- Grievance 9 62
- Grievance 10 64
- Grievance 11 66
- Grievance 12 68
- Grievance 13 70
- Grievance 14 72
- Grievance 15 74
- Grievance 16 76
- Grievance 17 78
- Grievance 18 80
- Grievance 19 82
- Grievance 20 84
- Grievance 21 86
- Grievance 22 87
- Grievance 23 89
- Grievance 24 91
- Grievance 25 93
- Grievance 26 94
- Grievance 27 96
- Removed Section 98
- Repeated Injury by an Unfit Ruler 100
- Our British Brethren 102
- Colonial Emigration 103
- Enemies in War, in Peace Friends 106

Chapter 4: Resolution of Independence 109
- The Declaration 110

Contents

    Resolution of Independence.............................112
    Free and Independent States............................113
    Appeal to Divine Providence............................117
    Mutual Pledge 120
    Stephen Hopkins 123

Chapter 5: Signature Block.........................123
    Charles Carroll of Carrollton.....................126
    Richard Stockton 128
    Joseph Hewes...130
    James Wilson..131
    John Adams 133
    Francis Hopkinson 135

Chapter 6: Distribution............................137

Appendix A: Signatories by State 141
    Connecticut..142
    Delaware..143
    Georgia..144
    Maryland 145
    Massachusetts 146
    New Hampshire 148
    New Jersey 149
    New York...151
    North Carolina 152
    Pennsylvania..153
    Rhode Island 156
    South Carolina 157
    Virginia..158
    Others..160

Appendix B: Enlightenment Sources 163

Appendix C: Bibliography 173

Index 189

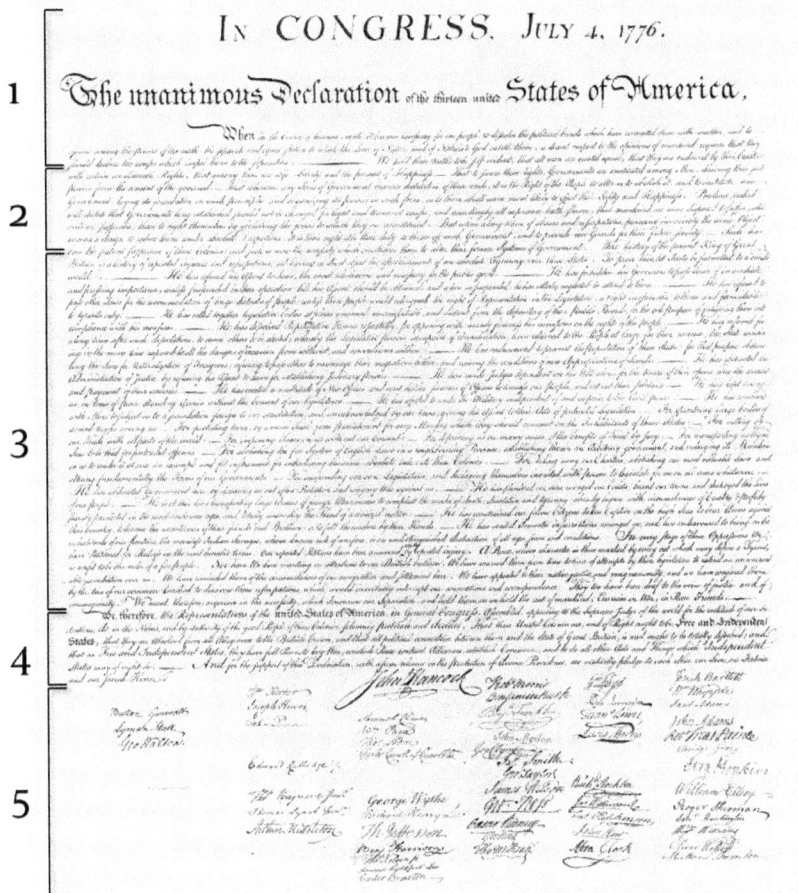

1. Origin and Preamble

2. Declaration of Natural Rights

3. List of Grievances

4. Resolution of Independence

5. Signature Block

INTRODUCTION

"It is not a matter of indifference that the minds of the people be enlightened."
—Montesquieu, *The Spirit of the Laws*

In perhaps the most memorable passage from the *Declaration of Independence*, Thomas Jefferson wrote, "We hold these truths to be self-evident, that all men are created equal, that they are endowed by their Creator with certain unalienable Rights, that among these are Life, Liberty and the pursuit of Happiness." Americans today accept these expressions of human identity as a form of political blood: always present within us, yet hidden just out of view until some attack or injury brings them to the surface. Those who possess American citizenship upon birth know the lifelong joy of those federally protected freedoms. And for more than two centuries, those born into more oppressive systems, the "huddled masses yearning to breathe free," have clamored to our shores, hoping for access to those same rights.

The expressions of our freedom printed in the *Declaration* have been an inspiration to hundreds of millions since they were first penned back in the late eighteenth century. But as with most beneficial elements available in abundance, and at little cost to the recipients, the temptation to take these liberties for granted is overwhelming. Such passive sentiments have long been a concern. President Truman, speaking less than a decade after America achieved a worldwide military victory, cautioned the nation against this species of apathy. "We find it hard to believe," said Truman at a dedication ceremony for the National Archives building that currently houses both the *Declaration* and the US Constitution, "that liberty could ever be lost in this country. But it can be lost, and it will be, if the time ever comes when these documents are regarded not as the supreme expression of our profound belief, but merely as curiosities in glass cases."[1]

President Truman's concerns harken back thousands of years, to the warnings Moses gave the Israelites just before they crossed into the Promised Land. If the stories in Exodus are to be believed, there should have been no people more inclined to abide in their faith than the Israelites. Here was a nation rescued from slavery by God himself, and led by a literal pillar of fire through the parted waters of the Red Sea. But those events were forty years in the past, and Moses knew that the people were prone to stray. Calling them back to the promises and commands of God, he implored his hearers to "fix these words of mine in your hearts and minds; tie them as symbols on your hands and bind them on your foreheads. Teach them to your children, talking about them when you sit at home and when you walk along the road, when you lie down and when you get up. Write them on the doorframes of your houses and on your gates, so that your days and the days of your children may be many in the land the Lord swore to give your ancestors, as many as the days that the heavens are above the earth."[2]

---

1 Harry S. Truman, "Address at the National Archives Dedicating the New Shrine for the Declaration of Independence, the Constitution, and the Bill of Rights," December 15, 1952, in *The American Presidency Project*, http://www.presidency.ucsb.edu/ws/?pid=14358.
2 Deuteronomy 11:18-21 (New International Version).

Introduction

xiii

The *Declaration of Independence* is the closest thing that the secular government of the United States has to the promises of God. But it's not enough for that charter to just sit there in the National Archives Rotunda; it was designed to get out and move among the people. The natural rights it describes should be fixed in our hearts and minds, and taught to our children. We should speak of them when we sit at home, and when we walk along the road, so essential are they to our liberty and national existence. Yet we live today in extraordinarily unenlightened times. We send more people into college than ever, yet produce fewer scholars. We have access to the most technologically advanced tools the world has ever seen, yet most have virtually no understanding of elementary science. Our connected devices give us unparalleled access to the whole of human knowledge, yet our minds contain little more than the key plotlines from *Game of Thrones*.

Francis Hopkinson, one of the signers of the *Declaration*, claimed that the typical American of his day "reads political disquisitions and learns the great outlines of his rights as a man and as a citizen."[3] Perhaps he overstated things a bit. And yet, we understand instinctively that America's political leaders from the colonial era produced something that is beyond the creative grasp of our present elected officials. The Second Continental Congress that ratified the *Declaration* benefited from having geniuses like Jefferson and Benjamin Franklin in their midst. But they also had something more, something that Jefferson called the "harmonizing sentiments of the day."[4]

---

3   Francis Hopkinson, "Translation of a Letter, written by a Foreigner on his Travels," in *A Library of American Literature: Literature of the Revolutionary Period*, ed. Edmund Clarence Stedman and Ellen Mackay Hutchinson (New York: Charles L. Webster & Co., 1888), 3:236-240.

4   Thomas Jefferson to Henry Lee, Monticello, May 8, 1825, in *Founders Online: The Papers of Thomas Jefferson*, National Archives, http://founders.archives.

Those harmonizing sentiments hung in the colonial air thanks to the *Enlightenment*, a period of intellectual, scientific, and political growth that dominated much of the eighteenth century. While our natural rights have always existed—the Creator, after all, endowed us with the benefits of life, liberty, and the pursuit of happiness—the Enlightenment writers possessed the philosophical depth to understand these rights, and communicated them through books and pamphlets that eventually transformed the world. They did it all in a time without the internet, without high-speed communications, and without modern comforts such as electric lights, lending libraries, or accommodating heads of state.

Applying those ideals in the face of an out-of-control Parliament and an overbearing monarch was not an easy task, nor a safe one. The basic truths coming out of the Enlightenment were not always popular—at least one key liberty-minded author was sentenced to death for suggesting that the people had more authority than the king.[5] The founders understood the risks, but they also understood that they could not "doze, or set supinely indifferent on the brink of Destruction, while the Iron Hand of Oppression is daily tearing the choicest Fruit from the fair Tree of Liberty."[6]

That generation proved themselves worthy to the cause of liberty, and we are the direct beneficiaries of their bravery. While few Americans today may read political disquisitions, the sources that Jefferson and his fellow compatriots used to inform George III of his lost American colonies still exist today. And thanks to the very freedoms those sources promised, we have unparalleled access to those works, the freedom of speech with which to discuss

---

gov/documents/Jefferson/98-01-02-5212.
5 Algernon Sidney (1623-1683), author of *Discourses Concerning Government*.
6 "A Letter of Correspondence, to the other Towns," Boston, November 20, 1772, in *The Votes and Proceedings of the Freeholders and other Inhabitants of the Town of Boston* (Boston: Edes and Gill, 1772), 34.

them openly, and the benefits of the founders' thoughts to guide us through some of the more complex portions.

This book offers an introductory look at some of the most important and influential of those sources, some stretching clear back to the founding of Western civilization. The *Declaration of Independence*, with its cogent summaries of Enlightenment ideals, provides the foundation for this grand tour. As we pass through each sentence and clause of its text, we'll investigate the primary sources and historical events that Thomas Jefferson and the other congressional delegates relied on to craft that treasonous document.

The *Declaration* content printed in this book comes from the engrossed copy that most of us are familiar with today, the one that the signers attached their names to in boldness and ink. There are other versions that predate this edition, mostly rough drafts provided by the Committee of Five to the full Congress. While there will be occasional references to parts of those earlier productions, most of what you read here will be from the official, ratified form of the text.

As for the primary sources that support the *Declaration*, you will encounter lengthy quotes from these works in their original forms, bad spelling and all. In some cases, especially when this book has relied on modern editions of those classics, relevant quotes may appear in a modified form, as passed on through those edited versions. For works originally in a language other than English, the format provided by the translator is employed.

Another archaic import comes through the various dates referenced throughout the book. The transition from the Julian calendar to the Gregorian calendar in 1752 resulted in the loss of eleven days, and a glance at any official colonial calendar from that year will include a foreshortened September, with the fourteenth day of that month immediately following the second. Some writers who published content after that change would retroactively adjust older dates by those missing eleven days, employing a "New Style" instead of an "Old Style" dating system. For example, although George Washington's mother gave birth to him on what she thought was February 11, 1731, we who live beyond the calendar adjustment celebrate his birth a bit later, on February 22, 1732.

But wait a minute—or a full week-and-a-half if you prefer. Washington was born in 1731, but moderns call it 1732. That's because of a second calendar trick in use between 1155 to 1752, where January 1 to March 24 of each new year (just before the feast of the Annunciation on March 25) retained the *anno Domini* of the year that proceeded it. And what's worse, these departures from the Julian and Annunciation calendar standards occurred at varying times across Europe and the colonies.

All this is to say that the dates included in this book rely on calendar norms used by primary and secondary sources relevant to each topic. That is, I punted. Most modern scholars will employ New Style dates, adjusted for Gregorian purposes, and shifting the start of each year to January 1. But if some post-transition author retained the Old Style dating system, I deferred to that expert.

While these caveats are like mother's milk to history buffs and computer geeks, myself included, they fortunately have little impact on the core concern of the book, which is: We need the *Declaration of Independence* now more than ever. The world seems to get stranger each year, and some days it's difficult to distinguish between frantic newspaper headlines and frantic social media memes. And yet, the *Declaration* remains, complete with its assurance that the rights we possess are not only natural and appropriate for invocation when seeking redress of grievances from the government, but they are entirely self-evident.

CHAPTER ONE

Origin and Preamble

The language and ideas that Thomas Jefferson placed into the text of the *Declaration* grew out of his long interaction with both literary classics and modern works by Enlightenment writers. Limiting the various influences on the document to written sources alone, however, would discount Jefferson's own intellectual contributions, not to mention the ongoing conflict that provided the *raison d'être* for crafting the work in the first place. Those immediate sources—the rising tension between the colonies and Great Britain, the power-altering Seven Years' War that ended a decade earlier, and the technological changes that made Britain even consider playing a larger role in American affairs from across an ocean—all of these and more were just as relevant as those monumental books in giving Jefferson the understanding of mankind's natural rights, and of how those rights play out in societies.

It is therefore instructive to take a quick pass through the history of the late eighteenth century as experienced in the New World. The opening lines of the *Declaration* provide a perfect opportunity for such a review, focused as they are on dates, authorities, and social structures at an international level. These elements, while often viewed as boilerplate and perfunctory to the main business of the text, nonetheless give the writing context and support. A similar document crafted by, say, the New York legislature a year earlier would have had a very different purpose and import, even if some of the components remained the same.

Origin of Authority
In Congress,

In modern American parlance, "Congress" is a proper noun that identifies the official legislative body of the United States, as in, "Can you believe what Congress did this time?" But in the opening words of the *Declaration*, the term appears within a standalone prepositional phrase. It's not a passive, descriptive term, but an expression of action, whereby the individual colonies sent forth delegates of their own choosing into a representative assembly, "in Congress," for a specific active purpose, and under the authority granted by those delegating colonies. The power vested in the Second Continental Congress to make decisions in the name of the thirteen colonies, decisions as drastic and permanent as separation from the empire of Great Britain, is an indirect power derived from those same colonies.

Although Jefferson will address the meaty topic of how governmental power derives from the "consent of the governed" in an upcoming paragraph, these two opening words provide an appetizer, preparing the reader's political and intellectual palate for the full course to come. In this innocent, almost throw-away line about the type of intercolonial gathering that produced the document, the Continental Congress is already establishing the true source of authority for independence: the people. The human vitality of the Congress is found in its delegates, who were selected by the representative bodies of each colony or plantation, which in turn were called and elected by the enfranchised citizens of those colonies. That is, by the people.

This idea that the people are the source of a political region's power was not universally accepted, but had solid support in England and its American colonies. Even King George and the Parliament accepted it as a given, since it was one of the conceptual supports for the English Bill of Rights of 1689, where the monarch was found to be subject not just to law, but to Parliament and its House of Commons, and thus to the people themselves.

For the men gathering in Philadelphia in 1776, there was perhaps no better presentation of this authority than John Locke's *Second Treatise of Government*. Locke wrote that men are naturally free and independent in a nongovernmental state of nature. But for their mutual benefit and protection, they voluntarily come together in political society, or commonwealth. "The great end of men's entering into society," says Locke,

> being the enjoyment of their properties in peace and safety, and the great instrument and means of that being the laws established in that society; the first and fundamental positive law of all common-wealths is the establishing of the legislative power.... This legislative is not only the supreme power of the common-wealth, but sacred and unalterable in the hands where the community have once placed it; nor can any edict of any body else, in what form soever conceived, or by what power soever backed, have the force and obligation of a law, which has not its sanction from that legislative which the public has chosen and appointed: for without this the law could not have that, which is absolutely necessary to its being a law, the consent of the society, over whom no body can have a power to make laws, but by their own consent.[1]

---

1   John Locke, "Of the Extent of the Legislative Power," *Second Treatise of Government*, 2.11.134, ed. Thomas Hollis (London, 1764), 312-313.

This wasn't always the dominant view within Britain. Before the Glorious Revolution in 1688, British monarchs advanced the notion of the *divine right of kings*, where God himself ordained the political legitimacy of the ruler, or more often, of a bloodline of rulers. This view placed the natural rights of some individuals— those in the royal line of succession—above all others. A toned-down variation of this right appears in *Leviathan*, the political theory of Thomas Hobbes.[2] Describing the nature of a commonwealth nearly forty years before Locke, Hobbes (who rejected a pure divine right of kings) identified the people as the source of political power, but advocated the permanent and unalterable transfer of that power into the hands of a Sovereign. While this political perspective was rejected by the time of George III, his reign came just a few generations after it ceased to be the norm, and those ideas from before the rise of William and Mary in the late seventeenth century would certainly have offered powerful temptations. Putting the *Declaration*'s opening focus on the Congress of the people places the entire authority for the decision of independence where the signers wanted it: with the people.

DOCUMENT DATE
JULY 4, 1776.

The Fourth of July is as American as apple pie, and the elation with which people celebrate the day even two centuries later rivals Christmas in the reverence attributed to it. When the delegates finally made a commitment to declare independence from England, John Adams felt such emotion over the cause that he wrote to his wife Abigail, assuring her that future generations would recall the day "with Pomp and Parade, with Shews, Games, Sports, Guns, Bells, Bonfires and Illuminations from one End of this Continent

---

2   Thomas Hobbes, *Leviathan* (London, 1651).

to the other from this Time forward forever more." Yes, that glorious day, "the Second Day of July 1776, will be the most memorable Epocha, in the History of America."[3]

Of course, we don't celebrate the Second Day of July at all, but instead reserve our excitement for July 4. But Adams's statement is not surprising, given the flurry of activity surrounding the decision for independence, and the multiple important actions and votes needed to reach the final, engrossed document. A quick review of the key dates and events leading up to the *Declaration of Independence* as we know it today is essential in understanding the environment and mindset in which Jefferson penned the core text of the document.

October 1066 • Norman Conquest of England

England's King Edward "The Confessor" died in January 1066, but the lack of a direct heir did not stop several powerful men from insisting that they deserved the throne. The subsequent battle for power included a string of invasions from regional kingdoms, with royal hopefuls hailing from as far away as Norway. Eventually, Duke William II of Normandy gained the upper hand and ascended to power, styled as William the Conqueror.

William did not come alone, but brought aristocrats from the mainland, who quickly displaced the vanquished Anglo-Saxon rulers. Some of the former residents sought friendlier environments in nearby lands, including Ireland and Scotland. Leadership, land ownership, language, culture, and the overall makeup of the nation changed significantly throughout the next several centuries.

---

3   From John Adams to Abigail Adams, Philadelphia, July 3, 1776, in *Adams Family Correspondence*, vol. 2, *June 1776 to March 1778*, ed. L. H. Butterfield (Cambridge, MA: Harvard University Press, 1963), 2:29-31.

June 15, 1215 • Magna Carta

Tensions between King John and rebel barons in the northern and eastern portions of England were quickly heading toward the military option, stemming in large part from John's harsh ruling style, his belief that royals were above law, and national financial losses in the recent Battle of Bouvines. The *Magna Carta Libertatum* was an attempt by the barons to impose restraints on the monarch. This contract established limits on regal power, and formalized the previously optional council of landowners that advised the king, a group that eventually became England's Parliament.

Although the peace established by the *Magna Carta* didn't last even three months, John's death by a sudden illness just one month into the battle led to acceptance of a revised charter under young Henry III. New variations of the document appeared over the centuries, though with the rise of a structured Parliament and a stronger monarchy, the *Magna Carta* took a back seat until the sixteenth century, when it was used to help argue against the divine right of kings.

April 10, 1606 • Royal Colonial Charter

James I granted the first two colonial charters for settlement in North America, in 1606. (An earlier charter issued by Elizabeth I to Sir Walter Raleigh in 1584 had ended in failure, with the death or resignation of settlers on Roanoke Island, in present-day North Carolina.) One of James's charters went to the London Company, authorizing its stockholders to establish a single hundred-square-mile settlement; the first wave of adventurers arrived one year later in Jamestown, Virginia. In parallel with the London Company's grant, the king also authorized the Plymouth Company to set up a similar opportunity north of those claimed by the Virginia group. It took them more than a decade and a reorganization of their corporation before they could establish a settlement in Massachusetts, in 1620.

The Crown continued to generate charters and land grants for various North American lands, with the last American charter issued to Georgia in 1732. Some modern states, including New York and New Jersey, were acquired by England through war with the Dutch, their initial structures stemming from non-British grants. Other states, such as the Carolinas and Maryland, were carved out of Virginia by royal decree and granted through letters patent as patronage to aristocrats and associates of the various kings. The last active charter, the one belonging to Rhode Island, ceased its authority in 1843.

December 16, 1689 • English Bill of Rights

The Catholic sentiments of James II, and his close ties with France, did not sit well with members of Parliament, who viewed the king's rule as an imposition of the Holy Roman Empire into the British Isles. When the king favored his newborn Catholic son over his Protestant daughter Mary (the rightful heir), the Tories in Parliament banded together with Mary's husband William of Orange to capture the throne. James II escaped to France with his wife in December 1688, a Glorious Revolution that installed William and Mary as co-monarchs.

To avoid a renewal of former abuses and foreign intrusions into British politics, Parliament passed the English Bill of Rights. The document defined the basic civil rights of British citizens, and established limits on royal power, subjecting some actions of the king to parliamentary approval. For example, the king could no longer disband Parliament at will, nor could he impose taxes without a vote of the House of Commons. The document also guaranteed trial by jury, the right to petition the king for redress of grievances, and a mandate for the free election of legislators. The violation of these and other rights by George III helped drive Americans toward independence.

1696 • *Board of Trade*

To assist him with the administration of his overseas dominions, William III established The Lords Commissioners of Trade and Foreign Plantations, a formalization of an advisory function dating back to 1622. Known colloquially as the *Board of Trade*, this extension of the king's privy council managed the Crown's American lands with an assumption of supreme authority and control. In the king's name, they altered charters, issued instructions to royal governors that rankled local legislatures and patriot citizens, and worked with Parliament to impose England's will on the American colonies.

1620 to 1789 • *Age of Enlightenment*

As the Renaissance drew to a close, a new era of scientific and philosophical Enlightenment began in earnest with Francis Bacon's formalization of the experimental scientific method, in 1620.[4] Advances in biology, chemistry, mathematics, and astronomy, made universal through the miracle of printing press communications, brought with it a parallel expansion in philosophical and religious thought. In the political realm, Enlightenment writers outlined a basic foundation of indi-

---

4   Francis Bacon, *Novum Organum*.

vidual and commonwealth rights, one that insisted on government structures under the control of the governed.

Many of the philosophical principles embodied in the *Declaration* stem from writings created during this Age of Reason, including works published right up to the Second Continental Congress. Some of the key works include Thomas Hobbes's *Leviathan* (1651), Algernon Sidney's *Discourses Concerning Government* (1680, the publication of which helped seal Sidney's royal execution), John Locke's *Second Treatise of Government* (1689), Montesquieu's *The Spirit of the Laws* (1748), Denis Diderot's multi-volume encyclopedia (1751–1772), and Adam Smith's *The Wealth of Nations* (1776). The Enlightenment came to an end with the French Revolution in 1789.

1754 to 1763 • *Seven Years' War*

The Seven Years' War, and its North American theater known as the French and Indian War, changed dramatically the relationship between England and its American provinces. The colonists were natural allies of the British troops fighting against French forces in New France (present-day eastern Canada) and the Ohio River valley. With the help of George Washington and other local generals, England won the war, and took over control of former French dominions on the continent. Thomas Gage, who fought alongside Washington and later became both the commander-in-chief of all British forces in North America and the much-despised governor of Massachusetts, rose to prominence in his role as the military governor of Montreal after the war.

Despite Great Britain's victory, the war's toll was enormous, especially the resulting financial burden. To help pay for the monetary outlays, Parliament imposed a series of tax bills on its citizens, including those in America who lacked a representative presence in the House of Commons. Some of those earlier bills were repealed, but not quickly enough to quell the rising American distaste for British meddling in what were viewed as local matters stemming from obvious civil rights.

October 25, 1760 • Ascension of George III

In the midst of a pan-European conflict, George III took over as monarch of both England and Ireland upon the death of his father, George II. The third ruler from the House of Hanover, and the first of this royal line born and raised in England and in English, King George III's reign included repeated military conflicts on an imperial scale. Despite the loss of its American holdings and the mental illness that plagued its monarch in his later years, England under George III exercised increasing world dominance, culminating in the defeat of Napoleon's troops at Waterloo in 1815.

March 22, 1765 • Stamp Act

In the aftermath of the Seven Years' War and its associated financial loses for the British Empire, Parliament passed the Sugar Act on April 5, 1764, to raise funds for the late war. Formerly, taxes in the American colonies were tied to the management and benefits of trade. Although it was imposed on a traded good, the Sugar Act represented the first large-scale law crafted specifically to raise funds for non-trade purposes. The Stamp Act, passed a year later, dispensed with the pretense of trade, mandating that a government stamp be applied at cost even to papers that never travelled outside the confines of a town or business community.

The taxation itself, while a burden, was not the core complaint raised by colonists. Rather, it was Parliament's assumed authority in imposing such laws over American dominions that angered the patriots. Without colonial representatives in the House of Commons, and in light of the dictates found in the various colonial charters, the Americans insisted that Parliament lacked a clear right to legislate on their behalf. The Stamp Act Congress, formed by the colonies in 1765, issued resolutions opposing both the taxes and the British claim of authority. Parliament eventually repealed both taxing acts, but simultaneously approved the Declaratory Act of 1766, which stated that the House had complete authority to bind the colonies to its laws "in all cases whatsoever."[5]

1765 • Quartering Act

During the French and Indian War, the colonies had been asked to provide temporary lodging for troops, especially when those soldiers were marching from Point A to Point B. When the war ended, those military laws began to lapse, and the law specific to New York, where the army kept its headquarters, expired just after the New Year, in January 1764. General Thomas Gage asked Parliament for some form of extension, and they delivered beyond his wildest dreams, passing a Quartering Act that essentially authorized a permanent standing military presence, and at local colonial expense.[6]

When the New York assembly refused to abide by the new law, Parliament passed a restraining act that suspend-

---

5   American Colonies Act, 1766, 6 Geo. 3, c. 12. Also called the "Declaratory Act."
6   Mutiny, America Act, 1765, 5 Geo. 3, c. 33.

ed the colony's legislature until it complied.[7] The legislators changed their minds before the suspending act took effect, but they never fully recovered from the harsh response by Britain, nor did the other colonies.

1767 to 1768 • Townshend Acts

The New York Restraining Act was just one of a series of laws designed to bring the colonies into compliance with the will of Great Britain and its Parliament. The four or five individual acts (depending on who's counting) contained within the so-called *Townshend Acts* were part of a program pushed by the British Chancellor of the Exchequer, Charles Townshend. The 1767 Revenue Act[8] set the expectations, with its return to a fiscal plan borne by American import duties. The Commissioners of Customs Act,[9] The Indemnity Act,[10] and the aforementioned act chastising New York rounded out the core set that came before Parliament prior to Townshend's death in late 1767. The final law, the Vice Admiralty Court Act,[11] which established military tribunals for violations of customs laws, passed in 1768.

These laws represented a sudden uptick in British control over the colonies, and the American response increased in parallel. Massachusetts sent out a *Circular Letter* to the other colonies in February 1768, in which authors Samuel Ad-

---

7   Rebellion in America Act, 1767, 7 Geo. 3, c. 59. Also called the "New York Restraining Act."
8   Duties on Tea, etc., Act, 1767, 7 Geo. 3, c. 46. Also called the "Townshend Revenue Act."
9   Commissioners of Customs Act, 1766, 7 Geo. 3, c. 41. The act set up a customs apparatus on the American side of the Atlantic.
10 Indemnity Act, 1767, 7 Geo. 3, c. 56. The act removed duties on tea imported from India, so as to compete with smuggled Dutch tea.
11 Colonial Trade Act, 1768, 8 Geo. 3, c. 22. Also called the "Vice Admiralty Court Act."

ams and James Otis argued against Parliament's authority to tax the colonies. When the legislature refused to recant the letter, Governor Francis Bernard dissolved the assembly, an act that did little to quell patriot frustrations.

March 5, 1770 • Boston Massacre

Along with the suspension of the legislature, Governor Bernard also oversaw the arrival of an increased British troop presence into Boston, ostensibly to quell the rioting of an unruly colony. Heated exchanges between the Redcoats and Boston residents were common, and in one boisterous and somewhat confusing incident in March 1770, British soldiers fired on and killed five protestors. Although most of the soldiers were acquitted through the legal efforts of John Adams, Boston never forgot the injustice.

December 16, 1773 • Boston Tea Party

While the 1767 Indemnity Act reduced duties on imported Indian tea, the parallel Revenue Act from that same year compensated for the loss in duties through new taxes. Since the colonists rejected the underlying authority of Parliament to pass such laws, some patriots and merchants responded to the laws by organizing a boycott against the India-sourced tea. A new Tea Act[12] passed in 1773 enabled the East India Company to import its products directly into other colonies, reducing the price further. But the hubris of Parliament passing yet another law without their input angered the Americans further.

On the evening of December 16, 1773, several dozen Bostonians assumed Mohawk warrior garb and dumped

---

12 Tea Act, 1773, 13 Geo. 3, c. 44.

more than three hundred crates of East India tea into Boston Harbor. England, naturally, responded with both force and legal remedies that made the Townshend Acts look tame.

1774 • Intolerable Acts

Those new acts of Parliament passed in the wake of the Boston Tea Party became known as the *Coercive Acts* within Britain, and as the *Intolerable Acts* on the American side. The first of the four laws, the Boston Port Act,[13] closed Boston harbor to most import and export ships until the colony paid for the discarded tea. To thwart the "open resistance to the execution of the laws," the new Massachusetts Government Act[14] voided the colony's charter, altered the means of selecting key colonial officials, and gave increased authority over the courts and legislature to the royal executive. Governor Thomas Gage used the act to dissolve the assembly later that year.

The third law was the so-called Administration of Justice Act,[15] which declared that certain crimes committed by officers of the Crown could be tried in Great Britain instead of in courts of local jurisdiction. On the expectation that the act would allow British officials to literally get away with murder, the colonists took to calling it the Murderer Act. An extension of the earlier Quartering Act[16] rounded out the four Intolerable Acts. This update enabled the commander-in-chief of the army and the governors of each colony, rather than the local legislatures, to decide when and where to provide housing for British troops on American soil.

---

13 Boston Port Act, 1774, 14 Geo. 3, c. 19.
14 Massachusetts Government Act, 1774, 14 Geo. 3, c. 45.
15 Administration of Justice Act, 1774, 14 Geo. 3, c. 39.
16 Quartering Act, 1774, 14 Geo. 3, c. 54.

September 5 to October 26, 1774 • First Continental Congress

The Intolerable Acts proved to be, well, intolerable for the colonies. To combat Parliament's abuse of authority, delegates from each colony (except Georgia) gathered in Philadelphia to hash out a unified response. In addition to a petition to the king for redress of grievances, the convention also crafted open letters for residents of Great Britain and British America (Canada), documenting the oppressions brought on America by the pretended authority of Parliament. Finally, the Congress formed a Continental Association, a trade boycott of British goods, which would remain in effect as long as Britain continued its overbearing actions.

April 19, 1775 • Start of Revolutionary War

While there had been violence between the colonists and the British military before 1775, a declaration by Parliament to George III in February 1775 that "a rebellion at this time actually exists" within Massachusetts altered the expectations and assumptions on both sides of the conflict.[17] On April 19, 1775, when hundreds of British regulars tried to capture and destroy munitions stored in Lexington and Concord, Massachusetts, the response by both parties was one of escalating armaments. Local militia units killed or wounded more than 200 British troops during the quick battle, with about 100 American losses. Thus began an intercontinental conflict that lasted through 1781, and officially came to an end when the belligerents approved a peace agreement in 1783.

May 10, 1775 • Second Continental Congress Convened

When the delegates at the First Continental Congress closed

---

17 Lord North (parliamentary debate, February 2, 1775), in *The Parliamentary Register* (London, 1802), 1:141.

their gathering, they proposed a follow-up meeting, just in case the king did not respond positively to their petition. Since things like sending more British troops, and engaging in battles with local militias, and passing more restrictive laws were viewed as negatives, the time eventually arrived for the colonies to reconvene, once again in Philadelphia.

The Second Continental Congress opened in May 1775. While we remember it today primarily for generating the *Declaration of Independence*, its delegates and committees performed numerous activities on behalf of the collective colonies, including acting as a central clearinghouse for the patriot side of the war effort. Congress disbanded itself at the start of March 1781, nearly five years after announcing the nation's separation from Great Britain.

December 22, 1775 • Prohibitory Act

If Parliament wondered whether the colonies were in rebellion before, the increase in military skirmishes, the boycott on British imports, and the establishment of unofficial legislatures in colonies like Massachusetts and North Carolina removed all doubt. In yet one more attempt to bring the Americans under stable British control, Parliament passed the Prohibitory Act,[18] which ended "all trade and intercourse with the colonies" until they should cease their traitorous actions.

John Adams confided to Horatio Gates that this law, publically approved by the king, essentially "throws thirteen Colonies out of the Royal Protection," making them independent of Britain long before the Congress had a chance

---

18 Revolted Colonies, America Act, 1776, 16 Geo. 3, c. 5. Also called the "Prohibitory Act."

to debate or approve such a separation.[19] When the delegates eventually embraced independence, the Prohibitory Act made the decision that much easier.

June 7, 1776 • Lee's Resolution

Richard Henry Lee, one of the delegates representing Virginia in the Second Continental Congress, brought forth a motion to the full delegation on June 7, calling for a decision on the matter of independence from England. The short statement proposed that the colonies be free and independent from Great Britain, and that they be "absolved from all allegiance to the British Crown." As discussed in chapter 4, some of the language from that statement found its way into the closing paragraphs of the final *Declaration*.[20]

While Lee's resolution was a succinct, clear statement of separation from England, the whole Congress directed that "a committee be appointed to prepare a Declaration to the effect of the said first resolution," which would provide time for some delegations to communicate the plan back to their respective colonies, and receive instructions concerning how they should vote on the proposal. The *Committee of Five* selected to draft the full *Declaration* included Thomas Jefferson of Virginia, John Adams of Massachusetts, Benjamin

---

19 From John Adams to Horatio Gates, Philadelphia, March 23, 1776, in *Papers of John Adams*, vol. 4, *February to August 1776*, ed. Robert J. Taylor (Boston: Massachusetts Historical Society, 1979), 58-60.

20 *Journals of the Continental Congress, 1774-1789*, ed. Worthington C. Ford et. al. (Washington, DC: Government Printing Office, 1904-37), June 7, 1776, 5:425, including content in Note 2 on that page. The original resolution, written by Lee and held by the Library of Congress, is found in the *Papers of the Continental Congress* (National Archives), no. 23, folio 11.

Franklin of Pennsylvania, Roger Sherman of Connecticut, and Robert R. Livingston of New York.[21]

June 28, 1776 • Draft Resolution Submitted

The work of drafting the *Declaration* eventually devolved onto Jefferson, since the other members "unanimously pressed on myself alone to undertake the draft." After crafting the document, he "communicated it *separately* to Dr. Franklin and Mr. Adams, requesting their correction, because they were the two members of whose judgments and amendments I wished most to have the benefit."[22] A few weeks later, on June 28, "the committee appointed to prepare a declaration, &c. brought in a draught" to the whole Congress, where it was ordered to "lie on the table" for an initial reading.[23] This edition, hand-written by Jefferson based on edits within the smaller committee, is known today as the "fair copy," and was the foundation for deliberations over the document among all delegates.

July 2, 1776 • Resolution of Independence Approved

On this day, the Congress voted on and approved Lee's earlier resolution for independence, with the journals that day documenting only minor differences in punctuation, capitalization, and spelling when compared to the original. The delegates, of course, had had access to the fair copy for a few days, but "not having had time to go through the same,

---

21 *Journals of the Continental Congress*, June 11, 1776, 5:431.
22 From Thomas Jefferson to Samuel W. Wells, Monticello, May 12, 1819, in *The Works of Thomas Jefferson, Federal Edition*, ed. Paul Leicester Ford (New York and London: G. P. Putnam's Sons, 1905), 12:306-309. Emphasis in original.
23 *Journals of the Continental Congress*, June 28, 1776, 5:491.

desired leave to sit again" until the next day, although that ultimately stretched into two days.[24]

July 4, 1776 • Declaration of Independence Approved

The review and editing of the document finally complete, "the committee of the whole Congress have agreed to a Declaration" on July 4, and ordered that it be printed and distributed to the colonies and the army. Two days later, the *Pennsylvania Evening Post* published the full text for consumption within the nation's largest city. Meanwhile, Congress resumed its business of executing the war on behalf of the colonies. On the same day that the *Declaration* was approved, for example, the delegates issued resolutions concerning the manufacture and transport of flint within the colonies—now states—and authorized the president, John Hancock, to hire another secretary.[25]

August 2, 1776 • Signing Begins

Timothy Matlack, clerk of the Congress and known for his adept hand, produced the engrossed copy of the *Declaration of Independence* on parchment, and presented it for signing by the delegates of each "free and independent state." Due to the pressing matters of war and independence activities within each colony, and the overall nature of political decisions, the full set of signers is not an exact overlap with those who voted for independence a month earlier. Nor did everyone who eventually signed do so at the August 2 gathering, though most did. A few signatories added their names over the successive weeks, and some historians believe that

---

24 *Journals of the Continental Congress*, July 2, 1776, 5:507.
25 *Journals of the Continental Congress*, July 4, 1776, 5:510, 516.

Thomas McKean, a delegate from Delaware, did not affix his name until 1781.[26]

DOCUMENT TITLE
THE UNANIMOUS DECLARATION OF THE THIRTEEN UNITED STATES OF AMERICA,

Although the *Declaration* had already received fair distribution across the colonies, including publication in prominent newspapers, Congress ordered "that the Declaration passed on the 4th, be fairly engrossed on parchment, with the title and stile of 'The unanimous declaration of the thirteen United States of America,' and that the same, when engrossed, be signed by every member of Congress."[27] The "unanimous" nature of the title was something new, since New York's abstention from the original vote back in July meant that unanimity was not yet a valid claim.

The approval of the *Declaration* by the complete set of colonies gave the document added strength, not simply because no colony rejected it, but because the full list included all of the larger and more influential players. It's no surprise that the Committee of Five selected to craft the *Declaration* had its members chosen from five of the top seven colonies in terms of population.[28] Virgin-

---

26 Gail Stuart Rowe, *Thomas McKean: The Shaping of an American Republicanism* (Boulder, CO: Colorado Associated University Press, 1978), 398, 429. Rowe quotes from McKean's last known letter, dated June 16, 1817, where he mentions a 1781 signing, though it is not clear if he is referring to the engrossed parchment.
27 *Journals of the Continental Congress*, July 19, 1776, 5:590-591.
28 The top seven colonies in 1770 by population (including a mix of slave and free residents) were Virginia, Massachusetts, Pennsylvania, North Carolina, Maryland, Connecticut, and New York. See "Population in the Colonial and Continental Periods," chap. 1, in *A Century of Population Growth: From the First Census of the United States to the Twelfth, 1790-1900* (Washington, DC: US Bureau of the Census, 1909), 9, table 1. For richer and more up-to-date population details, see Robert V. Wells, *Population of the British Colonies in*

ia was the most populous (including slaves, and by some counts, without them), and it was for this and other reasons of priority that John Adams insisted, "a Virginian ought to appear at the head of this business."[29]

The full convention likely included Robert R. Livingston, a key delegate from New York, in the drafting committee because he hailed from an estate along the Hudson River, and the full Congress coveted that province's approval. His clan supported the American desire for freedom, but the reasons had more to do with the family's treatment at the hands of New York Tories than a core desire to break away from Great Britain. Just a year after his placement on the committee, Livingston questioned his former role as a delegate, and wished "that the Congress would bargain away their Independency for Peace."[30] This lack of surety for the cause kept the provincial legislature from providing direct guidance on independence in time for the July vote. But despite this reticence, New York came around before the August signing, although Livingston himself had already been recalled, replaced by his nephew Philip.

PREAMBLE

WHEN IN THE COURSE OF HUMAN EVENTS, IT BECOMES NECESSARY FOR ONE PEOPLE TO DISSOLVE THE POLITICAL BANDS WHICH HAVE CONNECTED THEM WITH ANOTHER, AND TO ASSUME AMONG THE POWERS OF THE EARTH, THE SEPARATE AND EQUAL STATION TO WHICH THE LAWS OF NATURE AND OF NATURE'S GOD ENTITLE THEM, A DECENT RESPECT

America Before 1776: A Survey of Census Data (Princeton, NJ: Princeton University Press, 1975).

29 From John Adams to Timothy Pickering, Montezillo, August 6, 1822, in *Founders Online: The Adams Papers*, National Archives, https://founders.archives.gov/documents/Adams/99-02-02-7674.

30 Cynthia A. Kierner, *Traders and Gentlefolk: The Livingstons of New York, 1675-1790* (Ithaca NY: Cornell University Press, 1992), 219.

> TO THE OPINIONS OF MANKIND REQUIRES THAT THEY SHOULD DECLARE THE CAUSES WHICH IMPEL THEM TO THE SEPARATION.

Although this opening sentence has the overall feeling of, "May I have your attention please," Thomas Jefferson's "peculiar felicity of expression" shows through in every word.[31] This clause, one of the most memorable from the *Declaration*, is not simply a literary clearing of the throat, but instead communicates one of the key foundations of America's right to declare independence: political equality. The colonists viewed themselves as the righteously oppressed, but that on its own was an insufficient justification on which to embark on a nation-level separation from Great Britain. To become an independent state like England, one of the "separate and equal...powers of the earth," a society must possess the underlying authority to assume such a power.

For the delegates to the Continental Congress, that authority was available to the American people, not only by virtue of the charters that granted them access to colonial lands, but by supernatural right, a dispensation from "the Laws of Nature and of Nature's God." They made such claims the last time the colonies gathered together, in 1774, when they stated that "the inhabitants of the English Colonies in North America, by the immutable laws of nature, the principles of the English Constitution, and the several Charters or Compacts, have the following *Rights*...."[32]

The charters and land grants that established the boundaries and circumstances of each province offered a legal equivalency: the "bands which have connected them with another" were not

---

31 John Adams to Timothy Pickering, August 6, 1822. In the letter, Adams describes Jefferson's communication style.

32 "Resolutions declaring the Rights and Grievances of the Colonies," in *American Archives, Fourth Series*, ed. M. St. Clair Clark and Peter Force (Washington, DC, 1837), 1:910-912.

ropes by which a superior dangled a subordinate from the edge of a cliff. Rather, the link was between two peers, equivalent in their standing before each other and all mankind. Those charters were inviolable, though as detailed in one of the document's later complaints, Parliament was prone to modify and even dispense with those governing covenants, an action that assumed a hierarchical relationship, with England as lord and America as the serf.

As powerful as those charters were in defining the condition of the colonists' political situation, such grants were themselves subordinate to providential authority. In this view, it was not the king that received a divine right to govern, but the people, a right that brought with it an authorization, perhaps even a mandate, to establish a co-equal station whenever the existing sovereign power became abusive of that grant. Nearly two centuries earlier, the Dutch people had asserted such a right over Philip II of Spain, a prince who was supposed to be "constituted by God to be ruler of a people, to defend them from oppression and violence." But when the sovereign becomes the source of that oppression, "he is no longer a prince, but a tyrant," a change in relationship that authorizes the people to "not only disallow his authority, but legally proceed to the choice of another prince for their defense.... This is what the law of nature dictates for the defense of liberty, which we ought to transmit to posterity, even at the hazard of our lives."[33]

---

33 "The Act of Abjuration," translated in *A Fourth Collection of Scarce and Valuable Tracts* (London, 1751), 2:417. Originally signed by several states of the Netherlands on July 26, 1581. Historian Stephen Lucas argues that, while Jefferson may not have directly referenced the Dutch declaration when crafting the American variant, the influences of that earlier work found their way into other sources that Jefferson would certainly have studied. See Stephen E. Lucas, "The 'Plakkaat van Verlatinge': A Neglected Model for the American Declaration of Independence," in *Connecting Cultures: The Netherlands in Five Centuries of Transatlantic Exchange*, ed. Rosemarijn Hofte and Johanna C. Kardux (Amsterdam: VU University Press, 1994), 189–207.

CHAPTER TWO

Declaration of Natural Rights

In the beginning, God created natural rights. To the delegates at the Continental Congress, and likely to most members of the British Parliament, this Enlightenment understanding of mankind's native authority, instituted by the Creator himself, would have been accepted as a given. But assent and action are not the same things, and even in societies where the final authority of the citizenry is accepted as gospel truth, sovereigns have a vested interest in retaining power for their own purportedly benevolent purposes.

This tendency by temporal authorities to disregard the natural rights of the people was certainly not original to the colonial era. Although the application of these rights should have extended all the way back to Adam and Eve, potentates throughout history have scoffed at the very idea of their powers being subordinated to mere peasants. With this inclination in mind, it's not surprising that Jefferson opts to postpone the core arguments of the *Declaration* in order to teach a brief lesson in Enlightenment philosophy.

UNALIENABLE RIGHTS
WE HOLD THESE TRUTHS TO BE SELF-EVIDENT, THAT ALL MEN ARE CREATED EQUAL, THAT THEY ARE ENDOWED BY THEIR CREATOR WITH CERTAIN UNALIEN-

ABLE RIGHTS, THAT AMONG THESE ARE LIFE, LIBERTY AND THE PURSUIT OF HAPPINESS.

If any sentence in the *Declaration* stands out as the one to know, this is it. Even those Americans who have done their best to avoid learning and understanding the causes and outcomes of the Revolutionary War will likely have at least a portion of this statement on rights installed in their memory banks. It's quintessential Jefferson, and yet it's not. As you'll recall from the introduction, Jefferson never claimed that the ideas in the document sprang from his own fertile mind, but that they came from the "harmonizing sentiments of the day." Yet in this case, the word structure and pacing, at least as found in the *Declaration*'s first draft, have the harmonizing sentiments of a specific person: George Mason.

This fellow patriot and plantation owner from Virginia drafted that colony's *Declaration of Rights* just a few weeks earlier. The Virginia House of Burgesses approved and ratified that document's final draft on the very day that Jefferson started work on the national declaration. In the first of the Virginia statement's sixteen articles, Mason wrote that "all men are by nature equally free and independent, and have certain inherent rights...namely, the enjoyment of life and liberty, with the means of acquiring and possessing property, and pursuing and obtaining happiness and safety."[1] Assuming that Jefferson used this content as his starting point, he was still able to wordsmith it further, deftly trimming some of the excess verbiage. A few last edits by the Committee of the Whole, and the key replacement of "sacred & undeniable" with "self-evident" by

---

1   "Wednesday, June 12, 1776," in *The Proceedings of the Convention of Delegates, Held at the Capitol, in the City of Williamsburg, in the Colony of Virginia, on Monday the 6th of May, 1776* (1776; Richmond, VA: Ritchie, TrueHeart & Duval, 1816), 42-45. A preratification version of George Mason's draft appeared in the *Pennsylvania Evening Post*, on June 6, 1776.

Benjamin Franklin himself, left us with one of the most important and memorable summaries of mankind's place in society.

Whatever the original source of the sentence, the ideas it conveys are pure Enlightenment, especially with the focus on the Laws of Nature, a body of innate grants to humanity that the founders would have understood to be "permanent, invariable, and discoverable."[2] This was the work of the Enlightenment, to discover and take advantage of these facets of nature, made manifest by the Creator himself.

For Jefferson, this Creator was not any member of the Christian godhead, but the deistic God, the creator of all, including of all rights granted to mankind. The God of the deists was not capricious or arbitrary, instead choosing by his divine will not only to create useful and benevolent laws for humans, but for himself as well. This God "was subject, as it were, to his own laws, a constitutional rather than a Hobbesian monarch."[3] These ideas were not completely at odds with the Christian milieu of the day, enabling such bland monotheistic concepts to capture the hearts of even colonial Baptists. Consider, for example, the New Testament promise of God's mercy, that "their sins and their iniquities will I remember no more."[4] An omniscient God can, of course, remember whatever he wants. But he established for himself a boundary, a standard by which he would remember such sins no more, whether in actuality or in effect.

This type of deity, the kind that would bind himself, an all-powerful being, to rules and dictates, would not fail to create equally consistent, beneficial, and reasonable declarations for those he has

---

2   Clay Jenkinson, "Presidential Decorum," June 13, 2017, in *The Thomas Jefferson Hour*, podcast, episode 1238, http://jeffersonhour.com/blog/1238.

3   Charles Vereker, *Eighteenth Century Optimism* (Liverpool, UK: Liverpool University Press, 1967), 198.

4   Hebrews 8:12 (King James Version), paraphrasing Jeremiah 31:34.

created, or so thought those enthralled by the Age of Enlightenment. One of the Creator's most important grants, that of Reason, was "given men to bring them to the knowledge of God's will," according to the "Deist Bible" popular in that day.[5] Reason allowed these men to comprehend the grandeur of the creation, and invoke other benefits for individual happiness or social harmony.

The Creator endowed his benefits on not just a few hand-crafted humans, but on all of them, and in equal measure. So pervasive and universal is this distribution that it is considered a Law of Nature, an ancient thought mentioned by Aristotle in his classic *Rhetoric*. Human laws will vary from place to place, but undergirding them is a natural law, "something just by nature and common to all...even when people have no association or agreement with one another."[6] Because these gifts from the Creator apply to everyone in all places and at all times, they are fixed and permanent, and cannot be removed by the arbitrary will of any other person. Unlike temporal dispensations—fame, power, riches, health, and even basics like food and shelter—these essential rights are unalienable, because they come directly from God.

The Enlightenment writers, including John Locke in his *Second Treatise of Government*, tied this equal dispensation on God's part to the state of all humans in relation to each other. If God saw fit to provide his blessings equally to all, the implication is that those humans are, in fact, equal "in respect of jurisdiction or dominion one over another...without being subjected to the will or authority of any other man." Men are born "with a title to perfect freedom, and uncontrolled enjoyment of all the rights and privileges of the

---

5   Matthew Tindal, *Christianity as Old as the Creation* (London, 1730). The book was identified by some of Jefferson's contemporaries as the "Deist Bible."
6   Aristotle, *Rhetoric*, 1.13, trans. Michael Pakaluk (Princeton, NJ: The Witherspoon Institute, 2012).

law of nature." The problem is that such freedom and enjoyment as experienced by one person can impact, sometimes quite negatively, the freedom and enjoyment of another. Because of this, men "join in society with others…for the mutual preservation of their'lives, liberties, and estates, which I [Locke] call by the general name, property."[7]

The English jurist William Blackstone provided additional details on these rights. The right of life extended to "personal security," that is, "a person's legal and uninterrupted enjoyment of his life, his limbs, his body, his health, and his reputation." The right to personal liberty "consists in the power of locomotion, of changing situation, or moving one's person to whatsoever place one's own inclination may direct, without imprisonment or restraint, unless by due course of law." The final of Locke's three rights, that of property, is an "absolute right, inherent in every Englishman… which consists in the free use, enjoyment, and disposal of all his acquisitions, without any control or diminution, save only by the laws of the land."[8]

Jefferson, of course, replaces "property" with "pursuit of happiness." Locke himself used the expression in his *Treatises*, though not in direct relationship to the rights of man. While this quest for happiness may not have risen to the level of core rights for some eighteenth century authors, the concept was still discussed and written about, including by the theologian and Enlightenment philosopher William Wollaston. In *The Religion of Nature Delineated*, Wollaston identifies happiness as "the end [purpose] of society

---

[7] John Locke, *Second Treatise of Government*, ed. Thomas Hollis (London, 1764). The longer name of the *Second Treatise* is "An Essay Concerning the True Original, Extent, and End of Civil Government."

[8] William Blackstone describes these three rights in minute detail. See William Blackstone, *Commentaries on the Laws of England* (Oxford, 1765-1769), 1:120-141.

and laws," and that this happiness, together with truth and reason, conspire to "advance and perfect human nature." All laws and structures impressed on a society are just only to the extent that they are in line with truth, reason, and the pursuit of happiness.[9] When tyrants repeatedly erect barriers to this pursuit, they are obstructing justice, in the most basic sense of the expression.

PURPOSE OF GOVERNMENTS
THAT TO SECURE THESE RIGHTS, GOVERNMENTS ARE INSTITUTED AMONG MEN, DERIVING THEIR JUST POWERS FROM THE CONSENT OF THE GOVERNED,

In the years leading up to the Revolutionary War, many of Thomas Jefferson's contemporaries offered statements on the purpose of government that parallel this clause. Samuel Adams produced one such example in a report to the Boston town meeting in 1772, where he said, "The grand end of civil government, from the very nature of its institution, is for the support, protection, and defence of those very rights; the principal of which, as is before observed, are Life, Liberty, and Property."[10] Stephen Hopkins, a *Declaration* signer from Rhode Island, communicated similar sentiments back in 1764, recognizing that a desire for safety sometimes compels men to "forego some part of their natural liberty, and submit to government."[11]

---

9 William Wollaston, *The Religion of Nature Delineated* (London, 1722). For a discussion of this and other sources of the "pursuit of happiness," see Herbert Lawrence Ganter, "Jefferson's 'Pursuit of Happiness' and Some Forgotten Men," *The William and Mary Quarterly* 16, no. 4 (October 1936): 558-585.

10 "The Rights of the Colonists, A List of Violations of Rights and a Letter of Correspondence," in *The Writings of Samuel Adams*, vol. 2, *1770 to 1773*, ed. Harry Alonzo Cushing (New York: G. P. Putnam's Sons, 1906), 350-374. The document is more commonly known as the *Boston Pamphlet*.

11 Stephen Hopkins, *The Rights of Colonies Examined* (Providence, RI, 1764).

Although this idea was widespread in the mid-eighteenth century, the underlying concept that government exists to protect those it governs goes back to the foundations of Western civilization. Cicero, a politician and lawyer from the late Roman Republic, said, "*Salus populi suprema lex estou*," translated as "The welfare of the people should be the supreme law," and currently the state motto of Missouri.[12] While laws may exist outside of a constitutional form of government, they are most often recognized and realized when packaged within a governmental structure.

Other thinkers throughout the ages have clarified and adapted Cicero's words, even embellishing them, as Adams did, with an inclusion of Lockean rights. And since many of these writings came about as a warning against the overreach of strong government, it's not surprising that the foundational idea, that of government as a guardian, should remain. This protector is the commonwealth creature known as Leviathan, from Thomas Hobbes's book of the same name. The collective authority of the people, as embodied in their sovereign, "hath the use of so much Power and Strength conferred on him, that by terror thereof, he is inabled to forme the wills of them all, to Peace at home, and mutuall ayd against their enemies abroad," hopefully for their preservation and protection.[13]

By the era of the patriots, this protection was not just a background idea, but was codified in law, as explained by William Blackstone. In his commentaries on the law, Blackstone recognized that "every man, when he enters into society, gives up a part of his natural liberty." But he does this only for mutual protection "in the enjoyment of those absolute rights," namely, life, liberty, and the pursuit of happiness.[14]

---

12 Cicero, *On the Laws*.
13 Thomas Hobbes, *Leviathan*, 2.17 (London, 1651).
14 William Blackstone, *Commentaries on the Laws of England*, 1:120-141.

Failure of Government
THAT WHENEVER ANY FORM OF GOVERNMENT BECOMES DESTRUCTIVE OF THESE ENDS, IT IS THE RIGHT OF THE PEOPLE TO ALTER OR TO ABOLISH IT, AND TO INSTITUTE NEW GOVERNMENT, LAYING ITS FOUNDATION ON SUCH PRINCIPLES AND ORGANIZING ITS POWERS IN SUCH FORM, AS TO THEM SHALL SEEM MOST LIKELY TO EFFECT THEIR SAFETY AND HAPPINESS.

Although Jefferson here is invoking John Locke's formulation for the right of rebellion, the core understanding that citizens are authorized to oppose their prince has a long intellectual lineage. Some of this support came into the Enlightenment era through the religious writings of Thomas Aquinas. In the thirteenth century, that Catholic saint published a commentary on the writings of Peter Lombard, the Bishop of Paris from a century earlier. In Book 2 of his *Scriptum super libros Sententiarium* ("Commentary on the Sentences [of Peter Lombard]"), Aquinas analyzes the authority that God grants to secular rulers and governments, including the situations where that authority "may fail to derive from God."

After first making it clear that incompetent leadership is an insufficient justification for rebellion, Aquinas identifies the valid causes for opposition to the sovereign. The first, where the ruler came into power through usurpation or violence, did not directly apply to the Americas, though Jefferson is not hesitant to use terms like "tyranny" and "usurpation" for King George's actions against the colonies. But another circumstance hits closer to the mark, that of "abuse of authority." Aquinas says to be on the alert for state actions where "what is ordered by an authority is opposed to the object for which that authority was constituted." A straightforward example of this is when the king commands citizens to commit "some sinful action…which is contrary to virtue." But a variation of this involves failure to protect the citizens through the laws that were designed to defend them, bringing violence on them instead. In the wake of such acts, "not only is there no obligation to obey the authority, but one is obliged to disobey it, as did the holy martyrs who suffered death rather than obey the impious commands of tyrants."[15]

A few centuries later, Dutch jurist Hugo Grotius melded these ideas of just rebellion with the natural law sensibilities that would provide so much support to patriot ideals. In his book *De Jure Belli ac Pacis* ("On the Law of War and Peace"), published in Latin in 1625, Grotius identifies the valid justifications for a free people to initiate war against their sovereign, even invoking the writings of Scottish jurist William Barclay—a strong supporter of the divine right of kings—to bolster his position. "Those Princes who depend on the People...if they offend against the Laws, and the State, may not only be resisted by Force; but if it be necessary, may be punished by Death." Such actions are to be initiated only as a last resort, and only by a truly free people. But when the very survival of the people is at stake, when there is a "visible injustice... which no Good Man living can approve," even a conquered people may take action against the sovereign, though they must spare the king's life, a caution likely written in opposition to the French anti-royalist Monarchomachs, who advocated tyrannicide for unjust rulers.[16]

---

15 Thomas Aquinas, *Scriptum super libros Sententiarium* [Commentary on the Sentences of Peter Lombard], bk. 2, dist. 44, ques. 2, art. 2, in *Select Political Writings*, trans. J. G. Dawson, ed. A. P. d'Entrèves (Oxford: Basil Blackwell, 1948), 183.

16 Hugo Grotius, *The Rights of War and Peace*, bk. 1, chap. 4, *Of a War made by Subjects against their Superiors*, sect. 8, trans. A.C. Campbell, ed. David J. Hill (1625; New York: M. Walter Dunne, 1901), 372-373, 358. A portion of the quoted material comes from Fernando R. Tesón, "Hugo Grotius on

By the time John Locke was developing his social compact theory, the idea that a free people may rebel against their prince was firmly documented. Though Locke would certainly assign the right of rebellion to the people, he identifies the unjust sovereign or governmental power as the instigator of the rebellious actions: "Whenever the legislators endeavor to take away and destroy the property of the people, or to reduce them to slavery under arbitrary power, they put themselves into a state of war with the people, who are thereupon absolved from any farther obedience."[17]

Once the people have exercised their right of rebellion and removed both their sovereign and their structure of government, they return to a "state of nature," living as if no government presided over their lives. In this condition, they may, for their protection, reconstitute government and enter into a "politic society" of their own design, since "man has two powers: The first is to do whatsoever he thinks fit for the preservation of himself and others within the permission of the law of nature.... The other is the power to punish the crimes committed against that law." Such crimes may include the injustices of a tyrannical ruler.[18]

PATIENCE AND DUTY OF THE GOVERNED
PRUDENCE, INDEED, WILL DICTATE THAT GOVERNMENTS LONG ESTABLISHED SHOULD NOT BE CHANGED FOR LIGHT AND TRANSIENT CAUSES; AND ACCORDINGLY ALL EXPERIENCE HATH SHEWN, THAT MANKIND ARE MORE DISPOSED TO SUFFER, WHILE EVILS ARE SUFFERABLE, THAN TO RIGHT THEMSELVES

War and the State," *Liberty Matters* (essay series), *Liberty Fund*, March 2014, http://oll.libertyfund.org/pages/lm-grotius.

17 John Locke, "Of the Dissolution of Government," *Second Treatise of Government*, 2.19.222.

18 John Locke, "Of the Ends of Political Society and Government," *Second Treatise of Government*, 2.9.128.

> BY ABOLISHING THE FORMS TO WHICH THEY ARE ACCUSTOMED. BUT WHEN A LONG TRAIN OF ABUSES AND USURPATIONS, PURSUING INVARIABLY THE SAME OBJECT EVINCES A DESIGN TO REDUCE THEM UNDER ABSOLUTE DESPOTISM, IT IS THEIR RIGHT, IT IS THEIR DUTY, TO THROW OFF SUCH GOVERNMENT, AND TO PROVIDE NEW GUARDS FOR THEIR FUTURE SECURITY.

Although these sentences at first appear to temper the call for revolution in the previous statement, they are really just a continuation of the same argument. The fact that people are more disposed to endure suffering rather than to toss out key elements of their social and legal structures does not remove the core argument that those citizens are, nonetheless, fully endowed with the right to do so. This goes beyond the Thomist obligation to disobey unjust laws. The tyrannized citizens must not simply oppose the tyrant; it is their duty "to throw off such Government."

This insistence that the people rise up and engage in a *coup d'état* is shocking, not only because it appears to advocate bloody violence against the state and its rulers, but because the content on which Jefferson directly pulls these ideas is much more passive in its call for action. For these two sentences, though crafted with the same flair and expressiveness Jefferson instilled in the rest of the document, have as their birthplace a section from Locke's *Second Treatise*.

In the section of that work that deals with the "dissolution of government," Locke describes the willingness of people to put up with faulty governments to the point of tyranny.

> Revolutions happen not upon every little mismanagement in public affairs. Great mistakes in the ruling part, many wrong and inconvenient laws, and all the slips of human frailty, will be born by the people without mutiny or murmur. But if a long train of abuses,

prevarications and artifices, all tending the same way, make the design visible to the people, and they cannot but feel what they lie under, and see whither they are going; it is not to be wondered, that they should then rouze themselves, and endeavour to put the rule into such hands which may secure to them the ends for which government was at first erected.[19]

The "long train of abuses" phrasing is word-for-word identical—some might even say plagiaristic—but Jefferson's conclusion is much more aggressive than the "it is not to be wondered" theorizing provided by Locke. The people are not simply unable to see "whither they are going" troubled by the "prevarications and artifices" of the rulers. From the perspective of the signers, these people are reduced "under absolute Despotism," and made slaves in their own land until there is no future security. The Americans had already declared on several occasions to "the present and all future generations, that we have a clear knowledge and a just sense of [our rights and liberties], and, with submission to Divine Providence, that we never can be slaves."[20]

APPLICATION TO THE COLONIES
SUCH HAS BEEN THE PATIENT SUFFERANCE OF THESE COLONIES; AND SUCH IS NOW THE NECESSITY WHICH CONSTRAINS THEM TO ALTER THEIR FORMER SYSTEMS OF GOVERNMENT.

The patient sufferance of the colonies was well documented by the patriots, but the specific complaints and the level of angst varied

---

19 John Locke, "Of the Dissolution of Government," *Second Treatise of Government*, 2.19.225.
20 John Adams et. al, "Instructions Adopted by the Braintree Town Meeting," September 24, 1765, in *Papers of John Adams*, vol. 1, *September 1755 to October 1773*, ed. Robert J. Taylor (Cambridge, MA: Harvard University Press, 1977), 1:137-140.

significantly by region. Massachusetts and its major port city of Boston seemed to be in a never-ending battle for the future of civilization itself, while colonial leaders in sparsely populated Georgia expressed mixed feelings about whether opposition to Great Britain was warranted. Royal restrictions on westward expansion had a direct impact on North Carolina, Virginia, and other colonies that looked to America's interior as an opportunity for their growing citizenry. But Rhode Island, surrounded on all sides by other jurisdictions and an ocean, cared little about such constraints. Despite this mild indifference, its distaste for trade restrictions prompted some of its citizens to engage in the earliest armed battle against the British, several years before the Revolutionary War began.[21]

The varied application of British laws across the colonies was not necessarily surprising, given the differences in regional economics and demographics. But what irritated the colonies, to the point of revolution, was the *arbitrary* nature of the laws imposed on them by Parliament. Not only were the laws unjust, the claim goes; they were unjust because they were at variance with constitutional standards and natural rights. "No legislative, supreme or subordinate, has a right to make itself arbitrary," wrote Massachusetts pamphleteer James Otis, "but is bound to dispense justice by known settled rules."[22]

Concerns over the arbitrary abuse of government power arose during the English Civil War, more than a century before America's own rebellion. The Levellers, a populist movement during the reign of Charles I, issued a series of manifestos proclaiming the rights of the people, including the right to be free from arbitrary

---

21 In June 1772, Rhode Island residents attacked the British schooner *Gaspee*, a vessel used to enforce customs and cargo regulations.
22 James Otis, *The Rights of the British Colonies Asserted and Proved* (Boston & London: J. Almon, 1764).

rule. The leaders of the movement identified "the uncertaintie of our Government, and the exercise of un-limited or Arbitrary power" as the source of the "multitudes of grevances and intolerable oppressions" brought upon them. Their recommendation: "to abolish all arbitrary Power, and to set bounds and limits both to our Supreme, and all Subordinate Authority, and remove all known Grievances."[23]

Instead of making up rules at will, Parliament and the king were bound by Law itself to enact just civil laws, constrained by the Laws of Nature and key establishing documents. Edward Coke, Chief Justice under James I and author of the Petition of Right—one of the three key constitutional foundations of English law, alongside the *Magna Carta* and the 1689 Bill of Rights—declared that both the monarch and Parliament are subject to the law.[24] And "what that law is, every subject knows; or may know if he pleases: for it depends not upon the arbitrary will of any judge; but is permanent, fixed, and unchangeable, unless by authority of parliament." Specifically, "the pretended power of suspending, or dispensing with laws, or the execution of laws, by regal authority without consent of parliament, is illegal."[25]

Of course, the problem was not primarily that the king issued mandates in defiance of Parliament, but rather that these two agencies conspired against the colonists to strip them of their rights as British citizens. Therefore, the Congress deemed it necessary to fully dispense with the charade of British oversight in American

---

23 John Lilburne et. al., *An Agreement of the Free People of England*, April 30, 1649. Written on April 30, 1649, by four prisoners of the king being held in the Tower of London.

24 Edward Coke, Case of Proclamations, 1610 (neutral citation number 77 ER 1352, [1610] EWHC KB J22, (1611) 12 Co Rep 74). This case established the principle that "the King has no prerogative but that which the law of the land allows him."

25 William Blackstone, *Commentaries on the Laws of England*, 1:120-141.

affairs, and alter the underlying system of government that existed to protect the very rights presently attacked by King George.

CHAPTER THREE

List of Grievances

The *Declaration*'s list of twenty-seven grievances might as well not exist, for all the attention they attract from modern readers. Today, our eyes gravitate to the section on natural rights, with its high-minded talk of self-evident truths, and its uplifting message of life and liberty. The part at the end that contains the actual declaration of independence is essential as well, especially since the document's title pretty much requires such a section. But Richard Henry Lee's June 7 resolution calling for a vote on independence (see chapter 4 for details) already contained the bulk of that section's separation language. That short statement, if forwarded to King George and Parliament, would have produced a response every bit as violent as the one created by the full *Declaration* we have today.

For the congressional delegates, the introductory material and the final declaration were important. But the whole point of developing such a document was to reveal to a "candid world" the full slate of tyrannical abuses that prompted the colonies to seek independence in the first place. In 1776, the list of grievances was the essential part of the text, and without it, the colonies might not be able to attract sympathy and support from potential allies.

The text of the grievances consumes half of the full document's length. Fortunately for the Committee of Five, they didn't have to invent each grievance on the spot. The issues were well known to the delegates, in part because they had published them before. In October 1774, the First Continental Congress adopted several resolves, each targeting a different audience, but all listing comparable concerns. These missives culminated in the *Petition to the King*, which represented the first congress's official complaint of the abuses of Parliament.

Jefferson would have been familiar with these resolves, especially since their content derived in part from his own writings. Back in July 1774, a few months before the colonies gathered for the First Continental Congress, Jefferson developed *A Summary View of the Rights of British America*, a pamphlet that detailed the key concerns that Americans had with Parliament. That older document covers many of the same problems that found their way into the *Declaration*'s list of grievances, but with two key differences.

The first difference has to do with focus. Back in 1774, the colonies publicly blamed Parliament for what ailed them, and *Summary View* references specific instances of offending parliamentary legislation by name. Jefferson waxes frustrated over the violations of conscience brought about by "a body of men, whom [the colonists] never saw, in whom they never confided, and over whom they have no powers of punishment or removal." Two years later, the *Declaration* moves the blame away from Parliament, and specifically identifies "the present King of Great Britain" as the culprit.

The second key difference comes in the level of detail. To take just one example, the *Declaration*'s grievance 22, which begins with, "For suspending our own Legislatures," tops out at nineteen words. The related complaint in *Summary View* gets a nearly 300-word treatment. Jefferson provides page after page of documentation, with an extensive history lesson tracing the problem in part clear back to the Norman invasion of England by William the Conqueror, in 1066. The *Declaration*, by contrast, is short on specifics.

The 1774 document also spends much time fleshing out matters of trade, with mentions of the specific laws that brought about colonial woes. For example, the document shows how Americans cannot produce a hat from the fur of an animal captured on their own land, referencing a law passed during the reign of George II. The *Declaration* mostly forgoes quibbles over money, and instead lists issues of political excess in a blunt, terse format.

Jefferson had one more opportunity before the vote on independence to craft his list of complaints. His 1776 draft of the Virginia constitution, developed just a few months before his work on the *Declaration*, includes a highly edited set of grievances that is instantly recognizable to anyone familiar with the *Declaration*'s own list. Some sections are lifted word-for-word from the Virginia document for insertion in the one placed before the Second Continental Congress. And while the *Declaration* passed through the hands of an editing body before being released to the world, it never lost the textual heritage it found in Jefferson's earlier attempts at documenting Britain's abuses.

King George III, the Tyrant
The history of the present King of Great Britain is a history of repeated injuries and usurpations, all having in direct object the establishment of an absolute Tyranny over these States.

The Kingdom of Great Britain known to the colonists was one of ever-increasing might. The "United Kingdom of Great Britain" moniker hadn't been around too long, only since the 1706 Treaty of Union officially joined England and Scotland under a common government. But that first merger begat more, especially through the various eighteenth-century wars that extended Britain's reach well beyond its island home. Under the 1714 Treaty of Utrecht, Britain collected Newfoundland, Nova Scotia, and Gibraltar from France and Spain. It didn't gain much territory in the American colonies at that time, though the position of the other European powers was greatly weakened. This gave England the upper hand during the Seven Years' War. Britain emerged from that conflict in 1763 as a truly Great Britain, bringing into its fold much of Canada, all of Louisiana between the Appalachians and the Mississippi River, and parts of the Caribbean. The nation's control of India also grew when it defeated French forces in the 1757 Battle of Plassey, capturing the Bengal region. But while it was land-rich, these wars drained England's coffers, and it looked to America and the colonial tax base for rescue.

It was in this environment that George III succeeded his father to the throne. George was the third British monarch from the House of Hanover (all three named George), and the first born in England proper. His father and grandfather had been *laissez faire* leaders where Parliament was concerned, but George III took an active role in addressing the doubled post-war national debt. With America's distance from most of the war's carnage and its increasing position in world trade, the king didn't hesitate to use the colonies as England's personal checking account. The *Declaration*'s grievances enumerate the specific ways that King George and his Parliament worked to abuse the colonies to this end.

Yet not everything described in the document constituted a true usurpation. Several of the grievances were complaints about powers officially granted to the king, at least within the boundaries of Britain. The king had the power to (temporarily) dissolve local legislative bodies, veto laws (or refuse to assent to them), and station Redcoats within British towns even in times of peace. In these cases, the charges of abuse rested on the American's insistence that its states were not possessions of England, and therefore the king's dictates did not apply.

Parliament and its sovereign disagreed, and strove to impose their will on the colonies through the force of legislation. Oh, and guns. The Sugar Act, the Stamp Act, the Townshend Acts, the Coercive Acts, the Quebec Act; the Americans saw in each successive legislation the stripping away of their natural rights, the rights of personal security, personal liberty, and private property. "Every species of compulsive tyranny and oppression," said William Blackstone, "must act in opposition to one or other of these rights, having no other object upon which it can possibly be employed."[1] For Jefferson and the other delegates, the tyranny was not just compulsive, but absolute, as it impinged on not just "one or other of these rights," but on them all.

NOTICE TO A CANDID WORLD
TO PROVE THIS, LET FACTS BE SUBMITTED TO A CANDID WORLD.

The Congress hoped that by declaring independence, it could entice other nations to rush to America's aid, something that "Free and Independent States" like France would never do if the colonies were mere possessions of Great Britain. It seems reasonable that these nations comprise the "candid world" to which Congress submitted its facts.

However, the European continent and its leaders could hardly be called candid. France, Austria, Prussia, Denmark, the Holy Roman Empire; these regimes were not brutal by historical standards, but leaders such as Joseph II in Austria and Catherine the Great in Russia were monarchs, and more than monarchs in their un-

---

1   William Blackstone, *Commentaries on the Laws of England* (Oxford, 1765-1769), 1:141.

derstanding of authority. It's unlikely that such rulers would have accepted the supposedly candid opinion that they governed at the behest of their citizens, and could be deposed from power if the masses wished it—though France's Louis XVI would come to this realization, reluctantly, soon enough.

The British sovereign, the assumed target of Congress's publication, also lacked the type of candidness for facts mentioned here. One has to wonder why Jefferson even bothered to bring this list up for review. The first Congress two years earlier had compiled a similar collection of "facts" for British review, but to no avail. Jefferson himself pondered the futility of such listings, asking almost exactly one year earlier, "Why should we enumerate our injuries in detail? By one statute it is declared, that parliament can 'of right make laws to bind us in all cases whatsoever.' What is to defend us against so enormous, so unlimited a power?"[2]

Given this oppression of opinion, the candid world may very well have been the good citizens of those states seeking to be free and independent. The call for separation from Britain, while growing, was by no means universal. Some key players were on the independence fence, and an official statement by their continental body might be the very tool to move them from the loyalist camp to the patriot side. It should come as no surprise, then, that the very first act of Congress after approving the *Declaration* text on July 4 was to call for its dissemination among the several states.

> Ordered, That the declaration be authenticated and printed. That the committee appointed to prepare the declaration, superintend and correct the press. That copies of the declaration be sent to the several as-

---

2 Thomas Jefferson and John Dickinson, "Declaration of the Causes and Necessity of Taking Up Arms, July 6, 1775" in *Documents Illustrative of the Formation of the Union of the American States*, ed. Charles C. Tansill (Washington, DC: Government Printing Office, 1927), 10-17.

semblies, conventions and committees, or councils of safety, and to the several commanding officers of the continental troops; that it be proclaimed in each of the United States, and at the head of the army.[3]

These instructions didn't once mention Britain.

GRIEVANCE 1
HE HAS REFUSED HIS ASSENT TO LAWS, THE MOST WHOLESOME AND NECESSARY FOR THE PUBLIC GOOD.

The *royal disallowance*, also known as the king's negative, provided a check on laws passed within the colonies. By refusing his assent, the king (or by extension, his privy council) could nullify an existing law, including those "most wholesome and necessary for the public good." Different from a *royal veto*, which could prevent a new law from going into effect in the first place, the royal disallowance applied to laws new and old, and through it the sovereign could dispense with any wholesome and necessary law he deemed abhorrent.

The king hadn't always possessed such a broad power. The 1689 English Bill of Rights called the king's negative a "pretended power," and as part of the mandate covering William and Mary's joint sovereignty, Parliament declared that "suspending the laws or the execution of laws by regal authority without consent of Parliament is illegal." But as with so many restrictions on regal power, the ban was short-lived, at least as enforced in America. Far from illegal, George's counselors viewed "the negative which the Crown has reserved to itself upon acts of legislature in the American colonies" as an absolute necessity, "in order to prevent those legislatures ex-

---

[3] *Journals of the Continental Congress, 1774-1789*, ed. Worthington C. Ford et. al. (Washington, DC: Government Printing Office, 1904-37), July 4, 1776, 5:516.

ceeding the bounds of the authority vested in them by their constitution."[4] The purported goal was to help the colonial legislatures avoid laws that conflicted with the British constitution. In practice, the negative became a blunt instrument with which to whack away troublesome acts.

In theory, the disallowance didn't apply to all colonies, and for those charters that omitted this royal prerogative—Maryland, Connecticut, and Rhode Island, plus some that only later restored this power to the sovereign—the claim of usurpation may be a bit overstated. But by the time the Congress gathered for its second session in 1775, the negative had been imposed on laws from all thirteen colonies, "for the most trifling reasons, and sometimes for no conceivable reason at all."[5] When war finally arrived in the Americas, "every colony had had one or more laws disallowed," including nearly five dozen in Massachusetts alone.[6]

GRIEVANCE 2
HE HAS FORBIDDEN HIS GOVERNORS TO PASS LAWS OF IMMEDIATE AND PRESSING IMPORTANCE, UNLESS SUSPENDED IN THEIR OPERATION TILL HIS ASSENT SHOULD BE OBTAINED; AND WHEN SO SUSPENDED, HE HAS UTTERLY NEGLECTED TO ATTEND TO THEM.

Colonial legislatures were organs of the people, elected locally and given power to establish laws of regional import. The royal governors, on the other hand, served at the pleasure of the king, the "royal" part of the title making that clear. Oh, to be a king, invest-

---

4   From Lord Dartmouth (William Legge) et. al., to the King's Privy Council, June 13, 1766, in *The Statutes at Large of Pennsylvania from 1682 to 1801* (Harrisburg, PA, State Printer, 1896-1909), 6:609-612.
5   Thomas Jefferson, *A Summary View of the Rights of British America* (Williamsburg, VA, 1774).
6   Charles M. Andrews, "The Royal Disallowance," in *Proceedings of the American Antiquarian Society* 24 (October 1914): 345.

ed with the power to install political leaders over thousands and tens of thousands, and to dispense with the whims and whimpers of the peasants. In a battle of wills between the king's governors and the people's representatives, the king naturally assumed his authority over the rabble and their laws of supposed immediate and pressing importance.

While Jefferson lays the blame squarely on King George, the royal governors were often willing pawns. Lieutenant Governor Thomas Hutchinson, assigned to oversee the Massachusetts Bay Colony, seemed to take a certain pleasure in thwarting the will of the colonial legislature. In 1769, the assembly passed a tax[7] on "the Income or profit of any employment exercised in any Town in the Province,"[8] including "the Salaries of the Commissioners and other Officers of the Customs in America."[9] Without any sense of irony, Boston customs officers complained to the governor that "we did not consider that our Salaries were subject to such Taxation in America."[10] Hutchinson agreed, and when the Massachusetts assembly balked, he sent the issue up the chain. The Board of Trade, the king's personal management team over the colonies and an agency destined to get its own rebuke in a later grievance, issued instructions forbidding the governor "to assent to any Tax Act of the nature of those annually passed there, unless there be a

---

[7] "Acts Passed at the Session Begun and Held at Boston, on the Thirty-first Day of May, A. D. 1769," in *The Acts and Resolves, Public and Private, of the Province of the Massachusetts Bay*, ed. A. C. Goodell (Boston: Wright & Potter, 1869), 5:5-20.

[8] Richard Jackson to British Board of Trade, January 14, 1771, in *The Acts and Resolves, Public and Private, of the Province of the Massachusetts Bay*, 5:55.

[9] From William de Gray to British Board of Trade, February 13, 1770, in *The Acts and Resolves, Public and Private, of the Province of the Massachusetts Bay*, 5:54.

[10] From Charles Paxton, Henry Hulton, and William Burch to Lieut. Gov. Thomas Hutchinson, Boston, June 24, 1824, in *The Acts and Resolves, Public and Private, of the Province of the Massachusetts Bay*, 5:53.

clause inserted therein, exempting all persons from being taxed for the Income and Profits arising out of Salaries not payable out of Monies granted to His Majesty by Acts of the General Court of the said Province."[11]

This response came to the notice of Samuel Adams, the rabble-rousing patriot and Boston tax collector. Writing under the pen name Candidus, Adams said that the suspension amounted to "government without the least dependence upon the people... under the absolute control of a minister of state."[12]

GRIEVANCE 3
HE HAS REFUSED TO PASS OTHER LAWS FOR THE ACCOMMODATION OF LARGE DISTRICTS OF PEOPLE, UNLESS THOSE PEOPLE WOULD RELINQUISH THE RIGHT OF REPRESENTATION IN THE LEGISLATURE, A RIGHT INESTIMABLE TO THEM AND FORMIDABLE TO TYRANTS ONLY.

As the population of each colony increased throughout the eighteenth century, immigrants and more established families sought their fortunes westward, where abundant land and the chance for adventure provided the initial seeds of the American Dream. These new homesteads rose up beyond the official western edges of those colonial counties already viewed as the extreme frontier. As the fixed left sides of these districts gave way to imaginary extensions, the idea of reasonable local governance likewise stretched beyond credulity.

When the boundaries could expand no farther, colonies passed acts dividing these regions into smaller counties with their own

---

11 "At a Meeting of His Maj. Commissrs for Trade and Plantations," in *The Acts and Resolves, Public and Private, of the Province of the Massachusetts Bay*, 5:55.

12 Article signed Candidus, *Boston Gazette*, October 14, 1771, in *The Writings of Samuel Adams*, vol. 2, *1770 to 1773*, ed. Harry Alonzo Cushing (New York: G. P. Putnam's Sons, 1906), 250-256.

seats of local governance, and granting each new district the appropriate number of legislative representatives in the general assembly, giving residents of the new areas a voice at the provincial level. But in at least five colonies—New Hampshire, New York, North Carolina, South Carolina, and Virginia—the king disallowed the increase, not in the number of counties, but in the number of representatives making up each colonial assembly, so as "to prevent further deviation from the spirit of the Charter."[13] Some new representatives entered office anyway, after the legislatures conveniently left out any mention of new legislators in the enabling acts. But when the Board of Trade did notice a violation, it was not slow in reprimanding the lack of control by the royal governor.[14]

The situation in North Carolina provides a typical example. The royal colony had enhanced its assembly through the addition of five new counties, between 1768 and 1770. Governor William Tyron, acquiescing to tradition, agreed to add two representatives for each recognized town in these new districts. Josiah Martin replaced Tyron as governor in 1771, and when the time came to build a new county from constituent parts of Halifax and Tyrrell counties, Martin denied the request, citing royal instructions "on certain conditions from assenting to any Acts by which the number of the Assembly shall be increased."[15]

---

13 Thomas Hutchinson, *Strictures upon the Declaration of the Congress at Philadelphia in a Letter to a Noble Lord* (London, 1776).
14 Jack P. Greene, *The Quest for Power: The Lower Houses of Assembly in the Southern Royal Colonies, 1689-1776* (Chapel Hill, NC, University of North Carolina Press, 1963), 383.
15 British Board of Trade, "Instructions to Josiah Martin concerning the government of North Carolina [Extracts]," in *Colonial and State Records of North Carolina*, ed. William L. Saunders et. al. (Raleigh, NC: P. M. Hale, Printer to the State, 1886-1905), 8:513-515, Instruction 14 from the Board's February 6, 1771, letter, which Governor Martin refers to, appears on page 515.

The North Carolina assembly attempted to comply with the spirit of the restriction by keeping the total number of representatives the same, with Tyrrell County offering to deed two of its five seats to the new district. Governor Martin, a stickler for the letter of the law, rejected this overture as well, because "I knew not how far I might be justified in passing without a suspending Clause, an Act that abrogated an ancient charter privilege."[16] Despite the governor's reluctance, the citizens of North Carolina viewed him with some level of affection, and when the county eventually came into being in 1774, it bore the name of Martin, in his honor. But Jefferson was not among those citizens, and in identifying the offending actor, he was not opposed to calling the king or his royal governors "tyrants."

GRIEVANCE 4
HE HAS CALLED TOGETHER LEGISLATIVE BODIES AT PLACES UNUSUAL, UNCOMFORTABLE, AND DISTANT FROM THE DEPOSITORY OF THEIR PUBLIC RECORDS, FOR THE SOLE PURPOSE OF FATIGUING THEM INTO COMPLIANCE WITH HIS MEASURES.

In response to the duties and taxes imposed on the colonies by Parliament through the various Townshend Acts in 1767, the Massachusetts House of Representatives sent a document, now known as the *Massachusetts Circular Letter*, to the other colonial legislatures. Samuel Adams, as its author, argued that Parliament overstepped its constitutional authority in imposing taxes on the colonies, and in other acts, some of which find expression in the *Declaration*.

The February 1768 letter, though mild by 1776 standards, included a sufficiently blunt list of complaints, among which was the implication that royal judges and officials (including the governor)

---
16 From Josiah Martin to Lord Dartmouth (William Legge), New Bern, NC, April 20, 1773, in *Colonial and State Records of North Carolina*, 9:374-375.

who took a salary directly from the Crown were bound to engage in behaviors of dubious probity. Governor Francis Bernard, on behalf of the Secretary of the Colonies, Lord Hillsborough, demanded that the House revoke the missive. When they refused, Bernard prorogued the assembly.

When the legislators met again, it was under the watchful eye of Redcoats, "those seats of freedom and justice occupied with troops, and guards placed at the doors."[17] The following June, Lord Hillsborough ordered the legislature removed from Boston, ostensibly to protect the elected officials from the "licentious and unrestrained Mob."[18] The temporary meeting hall in Cambridge, four miles from the occupied capital, was not completely unusual, as the legislature had used it once in 1721 to avoid an outbreak of smallpox in Boston, and once again in 1747 after a courthouse fire. But what was once a safe place for emergency use was now "unusual, uncomfortable, and distant." There they remained until June 1772.

The legislature found itself once more removed from Boston after passage of the Boston Port Bill and the Massachusetts Government Act, in 1774. This time, the assembly ended up in Salem, and at almost fifteen miles from Boston and its "depository of their public Records," the word *fatiguing* suddenly became more appropriate. Governor Thomas Gage ultimately dissolved the legislature in October.

GRIEVANCE 5
HE HAS DISSOLVED REPRESENTATIVE HOUSES REPEAT-

---

17 "Journal of Occurrences," *New York Journal*, October 3, 1768.
18 From Lord Hillsborough (Wills Hill) to Francis Bernard, Whitehall, July 30, 1768, in *The Papers of Francis Bernard*, vol. 4, *1768*, ed. Colin Nicolson (Boston: The Colonial Society of Massachusetts, 2015), 271-274.

EDLY, FOR OPPOSING WITH MANLY FIRMNESS HIS IN-
VASIONS ON THE RIGHTS OF THE PEOPLE.

The decision to dissolve the Massachusetts assembly in 1768 came right from the top. In his instructions to Governor Bernard, Lord Hillsborough said that if the House refused to revoke the *Circular Letter*, "it is the King's pleasure that you should immediately dissolve them."[19] Whether the edict came from the king himself or an appointed royal officer, the colonists understood that this ability to eliminate the representative *vox populi* at will was not just an affront on natural rights, but struck at "the foundation of English liberty, and of all free government."[20] In rejecting the Crown's call to revoke the *Circular Letter*, the Massachusetts legislators insisted, "if the votes of this house are to be controlled by the direction of a minister, we have left us but a vain semblance of liberty."[21] The governor dissolved the assembly less than a week later.

Massachusetts wasn't the only colony, nor the first, to have its elected assembly abused in this manner. New York's governor dissolved its assembly repeatedly for daring to stand against the 1765 Quartering Act. When its legislature refused to comply with the law, on taxation-without-representation grounds, Parliament responded by passing the New York Restraining Act on June 15, 1767, one of the five Townshend Acts. The law prevented New York from passing any new bills until it commenced with the quartering of British troops. Not content to simply hit pause, Governor Henry

---

19 From Lord Hillsborough (Wills Hill) to Francis Bernard, Whitehall, April 22, 1768, in *The Papers of Francis Bernard*, 4:149-150.
20 "Resolutions Declaring the Rights and Grievances of the Colonies," in *American Archives, Fourth Series*, ed. M. St. Clair Clark and Peter Force (Washington, DC, 1837), 1:910-912.
21 "Message from the House of Representatives, to the Governor, June 30, 1768," in *Speeches of the Governors of Massachusetts from 1765 to 1775 [...]* (Boston: Russell and Gardner, 1818), 147.

Moore eventually dissolved the full assembly the following year, on February 6. At least nine of the thirteen colonies experienced similar disruptions in the years leading up to independence.

Beyond the power to dismiss a legislature completely, royal governors would also *prorogue* them, instituting an immediate stop on all legislative business. Prorogued members were still active legislators, and would resume new business once the governor called them back into session. Governor Horatio Sharpe of Maryland opted to prorogue his legislature after the *Circular Letter* affair instead of dissolving it, because "experience taught me that no step is so likely to attach the people to their representatives as a sudden dissolution." Though it appears less stringent than a complete dismissal, Sharpe used the prorogation as if it were a complete shutdown. "I shall not permit them to convene at soonest before next Spring," he told Lord Hillsborough, "so that, if your Lordship pleases to order it, they may be dissolved before another Session, at least they will have leisure to consider coolly the consequences that may attend their bringing on the Province His Majesty's Resentment."[22]

Jefferson rejected any authority by the Crown or its agents to dissolve legislatures. He used as evidence the fate of Robert Tresilian, England's chief justice under Richard II, from 1381 to 1387. Tresilian lost his head, literally, for suggesting that the king had the power to disband and reconvene Parliament at his pleasure.[23] Jefferson was so incensed at this assumed power of the Crown that in his 1776 draft constitution for Virginia, he declared that the

---

22 From Horatio Sharpe to Lord Hillsborough (Wills Hill), Annapolis, June 22, 1768, in *Archives of Maryland: Correspondence of Governor Horatio Sharpe*, vol. 14, *1761 to 1771*, ed. William Hand Brown (Baltimore: Maryland Historical Society, 1895), 506.
23 Thomas Jefferson, *A Summary View of the Rights of British America*.

state's executive "shall not possess the prerogatives of dissolving, proroguing or adjourning either house of Assembly."[24]

> ## GRIEVANCE 6
> HE HAS REFUSED FOR A LONG TIME, AFTER SUCH DISSOLUTIONS, TO CAUSE OTHERS TO BE ELECTED; WHEREBY THE LEGISLATIVE POWERS, INCAPABLE OF ANNIHILATION, HAVE RETURNED TO THE PEOPLE AT LARGE FOR THEIR EXERCISE; THE STATE REMAINING IN THE MEAN TIME EXPOSED TO ALL THE DANGERS OF INVASION FROM WITHOUT, AND CONVULSIONS WITHIN.

The dissolution of the Massachusetts General Court—the formal name for its colonial legislature—by Governor Bernard in July 1768 was just the start of a multi-year tussle over control of legislative power. Redcoats were already arriving in Boston Harbor in the wake of the *Massachusetts Circular Letter*, yet local resistance leaders still favored a diplomatic confrontation, a difficult prospect without an official assembly from which to issue petitions.

At a makeshift Boston town meeting on September 12 and 13, Samuel Adams, James Otis, Joseph Warren, and other leaders drafted a petition to the governor that reflected on "the critical State of the public Affairs, more especially the present precarious Situation of our invaluable Rights and Privileges, civil and religious," and humbly requested that "your Excellency would be pleased forthwith to issue Precepts for a General Assembly, to be convened with the utmost Speed, in order that such Measures may be taken as in their Wisdom they may think proper for the Preservation of

---

24 "Jefferson's Draft of a Constitution for Virginia," in *The Papers of Thomas Jefferson*, vol. 6, *21 May 1781 to 1 March 1784*, ed. Julian P. Boyd (Princeton: Princeton University Press, 1952), 294–308.

our said Rights and Privileges."[25] Governor Bernard denied the request, claiming a lack of clear instruction from England, and biding his time while troops shifted from Halifax and Ireland.

With "the Legislative powers, incapable of Annihilation" now formally rejected by the royal executive, Samuel Adams and his compatriots redirected their efforts to "the People at large for their exercise." They proposed a provincial "convention of towns" to meet in Boston's Faneuil Hall.[26] Not a legislature *in absentia*, mind you. The gathering's leaders were adamant that this was a voluntary committee, and passed a statement to that effect, renouncing "all pretence of any authoritative or governmental acts." And yet it engaged in House-like behavior, complete with parliamentary debates and the issuing of petitions to government officials. Everyone knew what it was, and that "it is not the Calling it a Committee of Convention that will alter the Nature of the Thing."[27]

The ninety-six town "representatives" assembled on September 22, and started on their core work of drafting a petition to the king for redress of grievances. In general, the gathering avoided the "inflaming Speeches" and "Treasonable Resolves" that preceded the event.[28] Governor Bernard nonetheless repudiated the body, reminding them that the "calling of an Assembly by private persons" was "an open attack on the crown's constitutional authority."[29] Even some of the invited towns struggled with the convention's

---

25 "At a Meeting of the Freeholders and other Inhabitants of the Town of Boston [...]," in *Documents of the City of Boston for the Year 1886* (Boston: Rockwell and Churchill, City Printers, 1887), 2:260-261.

26 John C. Miller, "The Massachusetts Convention 1768," *New England Quarterly* 7, no. 3 (September 1934): 445-474.

27 *Boston Chronicle*, September 26, 1768.

28 John Corner, captain of the *Romney*. See John C. Miller, *Sam Adams: Pioneer in Propaganda* (1936; Stanford, CA: Stanford University Press, 1964), 148.

29 *Boston Gazette*, September 26, 1768; and *Boston Chronicle*, September 26, 1768.

legality, with the town of Hatfield declaring it "unconstitutional, illegal and wholly unjustifiable…, subversive of government, destructive of that peace and good order which is the cement of Society, and [having] a direct tendency to rivet our chains, and deprive us of our charter rights and privileges."[30]

By the time Redcoats marched into Boston on October 1, the provincial congress had already disbanded, having forwarded their petition to their colonial agent in England. Governor Bernard eventually recalled the assembly the following spring, though its agitations triggered him to close it once more after just ten weeks, not to begin again until May 1770, and under a new governor.[31]

GRIEVANCE 7
HE HAS ENDEAVOURED TO PREVENT THE POPULATION OF THESE STATES; FOR THAT PURPOSE OBSTRUCTING THE LAWS FOR NATURALIZATION OF FOREIGNERS; REFUSING TO PASS OTHERS TO ENCOURAGE THEIR MIGRATIONS HITHER, AND RAISING THE CONDITIONS OF NEW APPROPRIATIONS OF LANDS.

For much of British history, citizenship was feudal in nature, and the Doctrine of Indelible Allegiance—the idea of "Once an Englishman, always an Englishman"—reigned supreme. Birth on British soil confirmed the citizenship claim, and allegiance was expected both to the Crown and to the lord on whose land you came into being. The king could also extend denizenship or naturalization through letters patent or outright conquest.[32]

---

30 "Answer of the Town of Hatfield to the Boston Selectmen," *Massachusetts Gazette*, September 23, 1768.
31 *Journals of the House of Representatives of Massachusetts*, vol. 45, *1768 to 1769* (Boston: Massachusetts Historical Society, 1976), vii-xvi.
32 A. H. Carpenter, "Naturalization in England and the American Colonies," *The American Historical Review* 9, no. 1 (January 1904): 290.

Beginning in 1350, Parliament made a series of naturalization reforms, initially to allow the children of overseas ambassadors to retain the citizenship of their parents. For the colonies, the most significant changes took place in the first half of the eighteenth century. An act under William III in 1700 allowed "Natural-born Subjects, within the King's Dominions, of Alien Ancestors" to inherit the British property of their parents, even if those parents were aliens.[33] Queen Anne, in 1708, extended naturalization to Protestants, bringing a wave of German immigrants into the dominions, including direct immigration into America.[34] While that law lasted only a few years, Parliament enacted a more liberal policy in 1740 that naturalized any foreigner who had resided anywhere in the empire for at least seven years, once the necessary oaths to king and church were applied.[35] These changes brought a wave of immigrants from the European mainland to America, especially Germans seeking a better life and real property.

Land ownership activated voting rights, and with those rights, power—German power. With many of the central and southern colonies expanding their labor forces by advertising access to land for new migrants, Parliament acted to quell what it saw as a rising and undesirable foreign influence. By 1760, nearly every colony had some form of royal restriction placed on alien land grants.[36] The shackled colonies found other inducements to bring in workers, including promises of a quicker immigration path, one where new citizens could engage in business dealings normally *verboten* to foreigners.

---

33 Aliens Act, 1698, 11 Will. 3, c. 6.
34 Foreign and Protestants Naturalization Act, 1708, 7 Ann., c. 5.
35 Naturalization Act, 1739, 13 Geo. 2, c. 7.
36 Cora Start, "Naturalization in the English Colonies of America," in *Annual Report of the American Historical Association* (1893): 323.

Beyond the Enlightenment-based arguments claimed by the Americans, some in Parliament were sure that the obnoxious colonial ideas related to taxation and authority must have a German root. George III, of Hanoverian blood and raised by German-speaking parents, had already reminded the nation during his ascension that he was "born and educated in this country, [and] I glory in the name of Britain," but imposing his British will on German immigrants couldn't hurt. In November 1773, he issued a decree to all royal governors limiting naturalization and divorce. "It is our expressed will and Pleasure," the act concluded,

> that you do not upon any pretence whatsoever give your assent to any Bill or bills that may have been or shall hereafter be passed by the Council and Assembly of the Province under your Government for the naturalization of Aliens, nor for the divorce of persons joined together in Holy marriage, nor for establishing a title in any Person to Lands, Tenements & real estates in our said Province originally granted to, or purchased by Aliens antecedent to Naturalization.[37]

Rhode Island and Connecticut, with their liberal charters, escaped this prohibition,[38] but the chilling effect on the other colonies was effective and intentional.

GRIEVANCE 8
HE HAS OBSTRUCTED THE ADMINISTRATION OF JUSTICE, BY REFUSING HIS ASSENT TO LAWS FOR ESTABLISHING JUDICIARY POWERS.

This grievance stems from a specific situation in North Carolina stretching back to the 1750s. The core issue revolved around

---

37 "Royal Instruction against passing Acts of Naturalization and Divorce," *Documents Relative to the Colonial History of the State of New York*, ed. E. B. O'Callaghan (Albany, NY: Weed, Parsons and Co., 1857), 8:402.
38 Cora Start, "Naturalization in the English Colonies of America," 323.

the source of authority for establishing judicial courts, be it the king, or the citizens of the province through their elected representatives. In post-constitutional America, with its three distinct branches of government, it seems strange that the judiciary served at the behest of the executive (the king, or locally, his governor) or the legislature. But the enabling language for the courts in colonial North Carolina appeared in legislative acts, pending the royal allowance, and backed up by the laws of England.

Various compromises concerning the establishment of courts appeared during the 1750s and 1760s, including the "creation of inferior courts and courts of oyer and terminer" by the Board of Trade. But the North Carolina legislature had insisted that the local county courts have jurisdiction over cases up to £50, something the British found of "too great Consequence and Importance to be adjudged and determined in these [lower] Courts," especially given "what must be the Qualification and Abilities of those who compose them."[39] The British, for obvious reasons, trusted the superior courts and their closer ties to royal authority, rather than the locally preferred county courts.

When it came time to renew the court laws in 1773, the legislature once again attempted to enforce its will, restoring the £50 threshold for the local courts, and granting local judges the power to attach liens against the English property holdings of those who had debts in North Carolina, even if the debtors had never visited the province.[40] The aspects of the law pertaining to superior courts

---

39 Great Britain Board of Trade, December 3, 1761, "Memorandum from the Board of Trade of Great Britain to George III, King of Great Britain concerning acts of the North Carolina General Assembly concerning courts," in *Colonial and State Records of North Carolina*, ed. William Saunders et. al. (Raleigh, NC: P. M. Hale, Printer to the State, 1886-1905), 6:587-591.

40 "Acts of the North Carolina General Assembly, 1773," in *Colonial and State Records of North Carolina*, 23:877, paragraph xxv.

were generally acceptable to the Crown, once the £50 threshold issue was resolved. But the legislators, who had "a peculiar proneness, to entertain the most illiberal, and sinister suspicions of [the British government's] measures," knew that the Board of Trade would never accept the increase in power for "the darling Establishment of County Courts,"[41] especially the extension of control over debtor property in "other Governments." And so they renewed both levels of court jurisdiction within a single act, hoping perhaps that the king would not notice the troubling clause. But the king did notice, and disallowed the entire act. In response, the legislature brought forth a new law establishing the county courts alone, without the offending superior court. Governor Martin prorogued the legislature before it could vote,[42] putting an end to that and all other pending legislation, and leaving the colony without a court system from 1773 until independence was declared three years later.

GRIEVANCE 9
HE HAS MADE JUDGES DEPENDENT ON HIS WILL ALONE, FOR THE TENURE OF THEIR OFFICES, AND THE AMOUNT AND PAYMENT OF THEIR SALARIES.

The Revenue Act of 1767, one of the Townshend Acts repudiated by the colonies, enabled a fleet of taxes that were designed, among other things, to make "a more certain and adequate provision for the charge of the administration of justice, and the support of civil government, in such of the said colonies and plantations where

---

41 From Josiah Martin to Lord Dartmouth (William Legge), New Bern, NC, April 6, 1773, in *Colonial and State Records of North Carolina*, 9:625-632.
42 From Josiah Martin to Lord Dartmouth (William Legge), New Bern, NC, December 24, 1773, in *Colonial and State Records of North Carolina*, 9:791-801.

it shall be found necessary."⁴³ While Parliament repealed all aspects of these acts—save a tax on tea—three years later, the Crown still had grave concerns about the financial dependence of its royal officials on colonial legislatures.⁴⁴ Indeed, several colonies had voted to eliminate gubernatorial salaries when those executives had spurned the representative will.

Some in England believed that the *Massachusetts Circular Letter* debacle, which stemmed from anger over the Townshend Acts, would not have gone as far as it did had Governor Bernard been fully independent of the legislature. So when residents of Rhode Island attacked and destroyed the British anti-smuggling schooner HMS *Gaspee* in 1772, Lord North decided the time had come to remove the fear element from royal decisions by adding not only governors but also high-level judges to the Civil List, the document that described for each colony which officials were to receive income from the Crown.⁴⁵

Rumors of this change trickled into Massachusetts in late 1772, prompting the General Court to investigate the claim. By the time November rolled around, the assembly confirmed that not only would the executive officers receive a fixed civil salary, "Fifteen Hundred Pounds Sterling annually out of the American Revenue for the support of the Governor of this Province independent of the Assembly," but also "the Judges of the Superior Court of Judicature...are to receive their Support from this grievous tribute.

---

43 Duties on Tea, etc., Act, 1767, 7 Geo. 3, c. 46. Also called the "Townshend Revenue Act."
44 William Griffith, *Historical Notes of the American Colonies and Revolution: From 1754 to 1775* (New Jersey, 1843), 54.
45 For some background on the Civil List, including how King George III brought stability to the list even in the event of the king's demise, see *Public Income and Expenditure*, pt. 2, *Gross Accounts of the United Kingdom, 1801-1869* (London: House of Commons, 1869), 637.

This will, if accomplish'd, complete our Slavery."[46] When the updated Civil List appeared in early 1773, it included the names of superior court justices, including that of Chief Justice Peter Oliver.

In addition to the salary issue, the colonists also objected to royal control of judicial tenure. Because the colonists believed that judges should receive their positions through an act of the representative assembly, they also understood that the legislature could dismiss court officials who exceeded their authority or in other ways disparaged the office. The judges, in this system, served *quam diu bene se gesserint* (during good behavior), which offered a limited though firm level of control over wayward justices. By paying the court out of the Crown's coffers, England had changed the situation of judicial tenure to *durante bene placito regis* (at the pleasure of the king). This update essentially offered lifetime appointments to judges, putting them out of reach of colonial legislatures,[47] and ending the "preservation of this Equilibrium" that came from legislative management of officer salaries and positions.[48]

GRIEVANCE 10
HE HAS ERECTED A MULTITUDE OF NEW OFFICES, AND SENT HITHER SWARMS OF OFFICERS TO HARRASS OUR PEOPLE, AND EAT OUT THEIR SUBSTANCE.

The grievance dealing with official harassment dates back to the very start of the conflict between Britain and its American colo-

---

46 Samuel Adams, "The Rights of the Colonists, A List of Violations of Rights and a Letter of Correspondence," in *The Writings of Samuel Adams*, vol. 2, *1770 to 1773*, ed. Harry Alonzo Cushing (New York: G. P. Putnam's Sons, 1906), 350-374. Also known as the *Boston Pamphlet*.
47 John Adams and William Brattle, series of letters, *Boston Gazette*, January 11, 1773 to February 22, 1773. The Adams portion appears in *Papers of John Adams*, vol. 1, *September 1755 to October 1773*, ed. Robert J. Taylor (Cambridge, MA: Harvard University Press, 1977), 256–309. Adams's February 11 letter discusses the tenure of justices.
48 Samuel Adams, *Boston Pamphlet*.

nies. The Molasses Act of 1733 provided an opportunity for the Crown to collect tax revenue from its dominions. However, the law was poorly implemented, rarely enforced, and the income derived from it and a related act from 1673 amounted to only about a quarter of the costs required to collect and administer the tax.[49] Three decades later, British debts from the Seven Years' War compelled Parliament to institute an improved replacement for the treasury-draining tax.

The Sugar Act of 1764 sought to solve the problems inherent in the molasses law. It reduced the actual tax rate on specific products to make it more palatable overseas, and provided better support and harsher fines for customs officers who previously believed "that without bribery and corruption they must starve."[50] The tax floundered in the colonies, partly due to resistance, and partly due to a troubled economy. Its repeal came soon enough, only to be replaced by the Revenue Act of 1767, one of the dreaded Townshend Acts. This substitute adjusted the rate for sugar even lower, but it also granted tremendous new powers to those perhaps still corrupt officials, making it

> lawful for any officer of his Majesty's customs...in the day-time to enter and go into any house, shop, cellar, warehouse, or room or other place, and, in case of resistance, to break open doors, chests, trunks, and other packages, there to seize, and from thence to bring, any kinds of goods or merchandize whatsoever prohibited or uncustomed, and to put and secure the same in his Majesty's store-house.[51]

---

49 George Louis Beer, *British Colonial Policy, 1754 to 1765* (1907; repr., New York: MacMillan Co., 1922), 230.
50 From Thomas Hutchinson to Richard Jackson, Boston, September 17, 1763, in *The Correspondence of Thomas Hutchinson*, vol. 1, *1740 to 1766*, ed. John W. Tyler (Boston: The Colonial Society of Massachusetts, 2014), 178-179.
51 Duties on Tea, etc., Act, 1767, 7 Geo. 3, c. 46.

The Commissioners of Customs Act, passed that same year, entrenched the tax collection apparatus on American soil. The Parliament insisted that the act was necessary for "the encouragement of commerce" within the colonies, but when combined with writs of assistance that granted officers carte blanche authority to enter homes and businesses, and to seize anything deemed illegal or customable, the new law had a chilling effect on the patriots. When abuses did arise, such as when goods were confiscated despite taxes having been legally paid, customs officers were presumed innocent, and the burden of evidence for paid taxes "shall lie upon the owner or claimer of such ship or goods, and not upon the officer who shall seize or stop the same."[52] Whereas customs officials were once seen as pesky and easy to deceive, they were now identified as "miscreants, blood suckers, whores, and Cossacks."[53]

History scholar Stephen Lucas notes that this grievance is the only one to invoke figurative language, with its biblical allusions to the swarms of locusts from Exodus 10 as the progenitors of the "swarms of Officers." Commissioners from the American Board of Customs were likewise linked to the "workers of iniquity" from Psalm 53, who "eat up my people as they eat bread."[54]

GRIEVANCE 11
HE HAS KEPT AMONG US, IN TIMES OF PEACE, STAND-

---

52 Certain Duties in the British Colonies and Plantations in America, etc., Act, 1763, 4 Geo. 3, c. 15. Also called the "Sugar Act."
53 Dorothy Denneen Volo and James M. Volo, *Daily Life During the American Revolution* (Westport, CT: Greenwood Press, 2003), 43.
54 Stephen Lucas, "Justifying America: The Declaration of Independence as a Rhetorical Document," in *American Rhetoric: Context and Criticism*, ed. Thomas W. Benson (Carbondale, IL: Southern Illinois University Press, 1989), 99.

ING ARMIES WITHOUT THE CONSENT OF OUR LEGIS-LATURES.

The French and Indian War—the American theater of the larger Seven Years' War—introduced a regular British army presence into the Americas, beginning in 1754. Not that the colonists were complaining. During the conflict, American militias allied themselves with British regiments, and one of the earliest skirmishes against the French involved a young major from Virginia named George Washington. When local hostilities died down around 1760, many troops remained. With battles in the other hemisphere ongoing for three years more, the presence of a stabilizing force was perhaps not initially surprising.

The war in North American ended officially on February 10, 1763, with the Treaty of Paris. But the troops stayed, at least some of them. Three months later, the passage of the Tea Act brought new meaning to the standing forces, as did the more powerful Stamp Act a year later. If the colonists had any lingering doubts as to the longevity of the remaining Redcoats, or their role in enforcing tax policy, the 1765 Quartering Act, with its requirement that Americans house and feed the troops, removed all illusions. As the colonies began their rebellion, the movement of British troops from Ireland and Canada into Massachusetts in 1768 made the standing army an everyday reality.

Animosity against the troops was both collective and personal. The First Continental Congress believed that "the keeping [of] a standing army in these colonies, in times of peace, without the consent of the legislature of that colony, in which such army is kept, is against law."[55] Their reasoning was one of sovereignty: America was not Britain, and therefore "his majesty has no right

---

55 "Resolutions Declaring the Rights and Grievances of the Colonies," in *American Archives, Fourth Series.*

to land a single armed man on our shores,"[56] not to mention the "ships of war" infesting colonial waters and impeding America's private shipping trade.[57]

Beyond the official objections, vocal patriots condemned the permanent military presence,

> composed of persons who have rendered themselves unfit to live in civil society; who have no other motives of conduct than those which a desire of the present gratification of their passions suggests; who have no property in any country; men who have given up their own liberties, and envy those who enjoy liberty; who are equally indifferent to the glory of a George or a Louis; who, for the addition of one penny a day to their wages, would desert from the Christian cross and fight under the crescent of the Turkish Sultan.[58]

GRIEVANCE 12
HE HAS AFFECTED TO RENDER THE MILITARY INDEPENDENT OF AND SUPERIOR TO THE CIVIL POWER.

Thomas Gage served as Montreal's governor during the waning years of the French and Indian War. At the height of the conflict, he had fought alongside George Washington in the field, and although his gubernatorial promotion was still a military position, he proved to be an adept administrator within the civil realm.[59] So it came as no surprise that George III would consider him for the

---

56 Thomas Jefferson, *A Summary View of the Rights of British America*. Some perhaps found it strange that Jefferson retained "British" in the document's title while simultaneous arguing that America was not Britain.
57 "Jefferson's Draft of a Constitution for Virginia," in *The Papers of Thomas Jefferson*.
58 John Hancock, "Boston Massacre Oration," a speech delivered in Boston, Massachusetts, March 5, 1774.
59 *Dictionary of Canadian Biography*, s. v. "Gage, Thomas," by Sydney F. Wise, http://www.biographi.ca/en/bio/gage_thomas_4E.html.

role of royal governor over Massachusetts in April 1774. What was surprising was the passage of the Massachusetts Government Act six weeks later.[60] The law, enacted with the other Intolerable Acts as punishment for the Boston Tea Party, essentially abrogated the Massachusetts Charter of 1691, and established martial law over the colony.

Where previously the Massachusetts assembly had appointed the various officers of the colony, save the governor, Parliament now believed that the General Court had, "by repeated experience, been found to be extremely ill adapted to the plan of government established in the province." The act granted the king, and by extension, Governor Gage, broad control over all essential aspects of governance and appointments within Boston and the larger Province of Massachusetts Bay, for "the promoting of the internal welfare, peace, and good government of the said province." Royal appointments thenceforth would no longer be in the hands of the legislature, but all executive officers, "counsellors and assistants, …judges of the inferior courts of common pleas, commissioners of Oyer and Terminer, the attorney general, provosts, marshals, justices of the peace, and other officers to the council or courts of justice…, sheriffs…, and the chief justice or judges" would now be appointed by the king, his council, or the governor.

The act also forbid any town to call its own assembly for any business (other than to fill empty seats), unless the governor first approved the agenda for that meeting. The military governor, starting in 1774, had nearly complete control over all civil officials in the executive and judicial branches, and he dictated the specific business of the legislature. The General Court disagreed with the law, to put it mildly, and when Gage dissolved their body in October, they simply declared themselves a new body, under the Massa-

---
60   Massachusetts Government Act, 1774, 14 Geo. 3, c. 45.

chusetts Provincial Congress name. While the military presence in Boston limited their authority in that city, they acted as the general legislature over the remaining towns in the colony.

GRIEVANCE 13
HE HAS COMBINED WITH OTHERS TO SUBJECT US TO A JURISDICTION FOREIGN TO OUR CONSTITUTION, AND UNACKNOWLEDGED BY OUR LAWS; GIVING HIS ASSENT TO THEIR ACTS OF PRETENDED LEGISLATION:

Having reached the halfway point through the grievance list, Jefferson now orients his pen toward Parliament. At issue is whether the British Parliament is authorized to pass legislation that impacts the colonies. As British citizens, those living in America had long acknowledged the English king as their sovereign. In fact, many of the charters establishing each colony or plantation commanded such "true allegiance to the King of England, his heirs and successors."[61] The Parliament garnered less respect, in many cases showing up in charters only as a way of clarifying which king the colonists should grant their allegiance to.

Beyond the granting of some early charters, England maintained little control over its American possessions before the end of the English Civil War in 1651. The Navigation Act, passed by Oliver Cromwell's government that year, brought the first hints of future domination. Other laws followed, including the Molasses Act of 1733. But America's great distance from the British Isles and the ease with which customs agents could be bribed meant that such laws had a relatively light touch. That all changed after

---
61 Lord John Berkeley and Sir George Carteret, "The Concession and Agreement of the Lords Proprietors of the Province of New Caesarea, or New Jersey, to and With All and Every the Adventurers and All Such as Shall Settle or Plant There," in *Documents Relating to the Colonial History of the State of New Jersey*, ed. William A. Whitehead (Newark, NJ: The Daily Journal, 1880), 1:101-103.

the Seven Years' War and Britain's sudden need for money. Soon, Parliament was passing tax laws, complete with a local collection system—and soldiers.

When the colonists balked, Parliament asserted its "pretended power"[62] by passing the Declaratory Act in March 1766. After reminding any and all that "several of the houses of representatives in His Majesty's colonies and plantations in America have of late, against law, claimed to themselves, or to the general assemblies of the same, the sole and exclusive right of imposing duties and taxes upon His Majesty's subjects in the said colonies and plantations," the act insisted that the "colonies and plantations in America have been, are, and of right ought to be, subordinate unto, and dependent upon the imperial crown and Parliament of Great Britain," and that this Parliament has the "full power and authority to make laws and statutes of sufficient force and validity to bind the colonies and people of America, subjects of the crown of Great Britain, in all cases whatsoever."[63]

The colonists rejected such authority not only because their charters and royal grants indicated local control over legislation and taxation, but because they viewed, or eventually came to view, Britain as a foreign nation. Just as England and Scotland had been distinct sovereign powers under a common king before the Treaty of Union took effect in 1707, the American colonies and plantations viewed themselves as united by virtue of a common sovereign, but distinct in terms of law.

---

62 Bill of Rights, 1689, 1 W. & M. st. 2, c. 2. This law was passed in response to the reign of James II.
63 American Colonies Act, 1766, 6 Geo. 3, c. 12. Also called the "Declaratory Act."

Grievance 14
For Quartering Large Bodies of Armed Troops Among Us:

Grievances 14 through 22 get specific about exactly how Parliament had violated the rights of British citizens in the American colonies. The first entry takes on an issue that was front and center in the minds of many colonists, especially in the central provinces: Britain's military presence, and its demand that each colony provide housing and daily provisions for the troops.

The quartering requirement stemmed from the French and Indian War of the 1750s, when British soldiers populated the Ohio River valley and other theaters stretching from Virginia to Nova Scotia. With the end of hostilities, formerly active troops retired to their barracks in the military-headquarters province of New York, where they became a tax-enforcement tool. In this capacity, military companies ventured out in formation across the province, and inhabited areas with larger populations, including New York City.

New York's own 1762 Quartering Act, renewed when the larger Seven Years' War was still ongoing, expired in January 1764.[64] With his soldiers marching out beyond the borders of New York proper, General Thomas Gage asked Parliament for legislation and funds that would provide for troops on the move. The Quartering Act of 1765[65] delivered this and more, legislating that provincial governments "quarter and billet the officers and soldiers, in his Majesty's service, in the barracks provided by the colonies," even when the troops weren't marching. If such barracks proved insufficient for the number of stationed Redcoats, they could be housed in "inns,

---

64 "An Act for Billeting and Quartering his Majesty's Forces within this Colony of New York," in *Documents of the Assembly of the State of New York* (Albany: Public Printer, 1913), 26:637-639.
65 Mutiny, America Act, 1765, 5 Geo. 3, c. 33.

livery stables, ale-houses, victualling-houses, and the houses of sellers of wine…, and all houses of persons selling of rum, brandy, strong water, cyder or metheglin," though not in private homes. While the law did provide some funding to pay for such billeting, any costs that exceeded this reimbursement had to be borne by the colonial governments themselves. In short, Americans would be required to pay new taxes to support soldiers already enforcing prior tax-collection laws.

In August 1765, just a few months after the king's approval of the new act, General Gage asked New York, via Governor Henry Moore, to provide quartering and funds for the troops. The provincial assembly reminded the general that a lovely compound for soldiers already existed in Albany. Gage put up with the rejection fairly well, but when it happened again a year later, Lord Shelburne, the prime minister, reminded Moore that "as it is the indispensable duty of his subjects in America to obey the acts of the Legislature of Great Britain, the King both expects & requires a due and cheerfull obedience to the same," and that while His Majesty was lenient with New York in the past, he will "not fail to carry into execution the Act of Parliament past last Session for quartering His Majestys Troops in the full extent and meaning of the Act."[66]

New York was comfortable paying for "the quartering Soldiers only on a March,"[67] but they refused to support stationed troops beyond their minimal barracks. Parliament grew tired of the rejections, and passed the New York Restraining Act of 1767, one of the loathed Townshend Acts, shutting down New York's as-

---

66 From Earl of Shelburne (William Petty) to New York Governor Henry Moore, August 9, 1766, in *Documents Relative to the Colonial History of the State of New York*, 7:847-848.

67 New York Assembly to Henry Moore, Albany, December 15, 1766, repr. in "Proceedings of the General Assembly of New York," *The Gentleman's and London Magazine* (May 1767): 267.

sembly until it complied with the Quartering Act. The province eventually fell in line in 1769, but when troops engaged Boston a few years later, the issue of quartering and billeting once again became fodder for agitation. Parliament passed one final Quartering Act in June 1774, addressing the case where "doubts have been entertained, whether troops can be quartered otherwise than in barracks."[68] The patriots rejected this and other Intolerable Acts, calling together the first of the two Continental Congresses to deal with the worsening crisis with Great Britain.

GRIEVANCE 15
FOR PROTECTING THEM, BY A MOCK TRIAL, FROM PUNISHMENT FOR ANY MURDERS WHICH THEY SHOULD COMMIT ON THE INHABITANTS OF THESE STATES:

Ebenezer Richardson, a Boston-area loyalist and customs officer—though that last role is unclear—shot and killed eleven-year-old Christopher Seider. The circumstances surrounding the death and subsequent trial are fraught with conflicts. Richardson was no friend to the patriot cause, and the common opinion was that "he was the most abandoned wretch in America. Adultery, incest, perjury were reputed to be his ordinary crimes."[69] On February 22, 1770, Richardson fired buckshot into a crowd of up to 300 youths who had conspired to identify and taunt area loyalist businessmen. While a jury found Richardson guilty of murder, Governor Thomas Hutchinson doubted both the correctness and fairness of the

---

68 Quartering Act, 1774, 14 Geo. 3, c. 54.
69 From John Adams to Jedidiah Morse, January 20, 1816, in *Works of John Adams*, vol. 10, *Letters 1811 to 1825*, ed. Charles Francis Adams (Boston: Little, Brown and Co., 1856), 204-210.

verdict. He obtained a royal pardon for Richardson, and hurried him away from Boston.[70]

Colonists in Massachusetts never quite got over Richardson's pardon and escape. So when Parliament passed the Administration of Justice Act in 1774,[71] with its promise of special treatment for those in the king's employ accused of murder, they lost no time condemning it as the "Murderer Act." As one of the Intolerable Acts passed in the wake of the Boston Tea Party, the "act for the impartial administration of justice in the cases of persons questioned for any acts done by them in the execution of the law" claimed to provide opportunities for a fair trial in those situations where any person working "in the execution of his duty as a magistrate, for the suppression of riots, or in the support of the laws of revenue, or in acting in his duty as an officer of revenue" just happened to commit murder or some other capital crime. If it seemed clear to the governor that the accused was guilty—not innocent, but "that the fact was committed by the person"—he could have the trial moved to another colony, or even to Great Britain for a hearing before the King's Bench.

Witnesses to the crime would be transported to the trial with their immediate expenses paid. But since those reimbursements did not cover any lost wages, the chance that a common citizen of Massachusetts would take a few months off from work, without pay, to make a round trip to the hostile seat of the British government seems remote. For Bostonians, it was Ebenezer Richardson all over again, this time perpetrated through a formal vote of Parliament, and enhanced to embrace the vilest of Crown employees, the "officer of revenue."

---

[70] John Adams, *Legal Papers of John Adams*, ed. L. Kinvin Wroth and Hiller B. Zobel (Boston: Massachusetts Historical Society, 1965), 2:396-411.

[71] Administration of Justice Act, 1774, 14 Geo. 3, c. 39.

GRIEVANCE 16
FOR CUTTING OFF OUR TRADE WITH ALL PARTS OF THE WORLD:

The grievance concerning world trade perhaps has the longest history of all the complaints, with its roots stretching at least to the Navigation Act of 1651, and possibly all the way back to the sixteenth century reign of Elizabeth I, long before any American colonies existed. The trouble was the British policy of mercantilism, alternatively derided as "the mercantile system" by no less than Adam Smith.[72] Under this system, an empire sought to maximize its economic power at the expense of all other world powers, using tax and trade policies that both helped and hindered its constituent states. High tariffs were placed on the import of manufactured goods, while raw materials enjoyed few import taxes, all with the purpose of increasing domestic manufacture and export of goods. Likewise, high tax rates applied to the export of raw materials, while you could send finished goods outside the country for little or no tax.

The original Navigation Act was supposed to be good for Britain and its colonies and plantations. Passed in October 1651 by the Rump Parliament (1648–1653) for the "increase of Shipping, and Encouragement of the Navigation of this Nation," the law declared that "no goods shall be imported from Asia, Africa, or America, but in English Ships."[73] Naturally, a government so empowered in the control of world affairs, and already telling Americans which ships they could use to sell their wares, could not leave

---
[72] Adam Smith, "Of the Principle of the Commercial or Mercantile System," bk. 4, in *The Wealth of Nations* (London, 1776).
[73] "October 1651: An Act for increase of Shipping, and Encouragement of the Navigation of this Nation," in *Acts and Ordinances of the Interregnum, 1642 to 1660*, ed. C. H. Firth and R. S. Rait (London: His Majesty's Stationery Office, 1911), 559-562.

well enough alone. New acts managing trade and tariffs *between* colonies soon appeared.

The Woolens Act of 1698[74] put severe restrictions on wool manufacturers in both Ireland and America, declaring that pretty much any wool-based product made in "any of the English Plantations in America" could not be "laid on board in any Ship or Vessell in any Place or Parts within any of the said English Plantations upon any Pretence whatsoever," nor could those products "be loaden upon any Horse Cart or other Carriage to the Intent and Purpose to be exported transported carried or conveyed out of the said English Plantations to any other of the said Plantations or to any other Place whatsoever." Selling wool within your own colony was still permitted, but exports had to be carried by hand with no help from horses, boats, or even river ferries. British authorities also clamped down on the manufacture and transport of American hats.[75]

A similar law restricting the iron trade passed in 1750. Billed as "An Act to encourage the importation of pig and bar iron from his Majesty's colonies in America,"[76] the promise of an open British market for raw iron was overshadowed by the other half of the law, which prevented construction of any new factories in the colonies that could process that iron, or that might turn that input into finished products. Existing foundries would remain, but a royal governor could shut them down at any time for being a "common nuisance." Merchants in England wanted to sell things made out of iron, and they didn't need the craftsmanship of Americans getting in the way. It was a loathsome mandate, and the colonists viewed it as "an Infringement of that Right with which God and

---

74 Exportation Act, 1699, 11 Will. 3, c. 13. Also called the "Wool Act."
75 Hat Manufacture Act, 1732, 5 Geo. 2, c. 22.
76 Importation, etc. Act, 1750, 23 Geo. 2, c. 29.

Nature have invested us to make use of our skill and industry in procuring the necessaries and conveniences of Life."[77]

GRIEVANCE 17
FOR IMPOSING TAXES ON US WITHOUT OUR CONSENT:

For Americans living in the twenty-first century, this grievance is the one that rings the most bells, with its rejection of "taxation without representation" and the expectation that the "consent of the governed" will be paramount in all legislative matters. Despite its primacy in our minds, this entry failed to make even the top ten in Jefferson's ordering. Yet it was a core complaint for the colonists, and although it was of more recent origin than the grievance on world trade, the imposition of unconsented taxes on Americans in the mid-1760s provided the foundation for so many of the other assaults on their freedoms.

The issue was not the taxes themselves, but consent by taxpayers, since "*Consent only* gives human Laws their Force."[78] Britain had imposed taxes on the colonies before that point, but they were limited to *external taxes*, which amounted to duties on imported goods. The Americans had not really raised any significant "objection to the right of laying duties to regulate commerce" by the Parliament. But they didn't have the same reaction to *internal taxes*, those imposed on goods and services created and traded within and among the colonies themselves. The argument against such taxes was straightforward: "A right to lay internal taxes was never supposed to be in Parliament, as [the American Colonies] are not

---

77 Samuel Adams, "The Rights of the Colonists [...]," called the *Boston Pamphlet*. See Indictment #9.
78 John Adams, "Two Replies of the Massachusetts House of Representatives to Governor Hutchinson," in *The Revolutionary Writings of John Adams*, ed. C. Bradley Thompson (1772; Indianapolis: Liberty Fund, 2000), 136.

represented there."[79] That is, in the absence of direct or representative consent, such taxes are prohibited. So when Prime Minister George Grenville pushed through the 1764 Sugar Act and 1765 Stamp Act with little consultation and no consent from British citizens across the pond, the colonies began their impassioned and relentless opposition to what they viewed as the arbitrary dictates of a foreign legislature.[80]

Detractors of this and subsequent revenue acts appealed to British law for their defense. The Enlightenment writer John Locke had said that the legislature "must not raise taxes on the property of the people, without the consent of the people."[81] His statement relied on principles that extended clear back to the *Magna Carta*, and were more recently voiced in the English Bill of Rights of 1689. The law was clear in that "no subject of England can be constrained to pay any aids or taxes, even for the defence of the realm or the support of government, but such as are imposed by his own consent, or that of his representatives in Parliament."[82] Since the colonists had no such representatives, they could not be taxed, at least not without grave consequences. Signer Stephen Hopkins viewed this truth as one of freedom versus slavery:

> For it must be confessed by all men that they who are taxed at pleasure by others cannot possibly have any property, can have nothing to be called their own. They who have no property can have no freedom, but are indeed reduced to the most abject slavery, are in a con-

---

79 Benjamin Franklin, in dialog with Grey Cooper. See Walter Isaacson, *Benjamin Franklin: An American Life* (New York: Simon & Schuster, 2003), 230.
80 Norman Wilding and Philip Laundry, *An Encyclopedia of Parliament*, 4th ed. (London: Cassell and Co., 1972), 300.
81 John Locke, "Of the Extent of the Legislative Power," *Second Treatise of Government*, 2.11.142, ed. Thomas Hollis (London, 1764), 323-324.
82 William Blackstone, *Commentaries on the Laws of England*, 1:135.

dition far worse than countries conquered and made tributary.[83]

GRIEVANCE 18
FOR DEPRIVING US IN MANY CASES, OF THE BENEFITS OF TRIAL BY JURY:

Courts of Admiralty enforced and prosecuted British maritime laws, especially the various trade laws passed by Parliament. Such acts covered the numerous duties collected for imported goods, and also imposed restrictions on transport by non-British ships and crews, especially those from France, England's enemy throughout the Seven Years' War. Smuggling was a common problem in Britain's overseas dominions, whether by foreign shipping interests looking to skirt British trade barriers, or by lesser crewmen looking to make a few extra shillings by bringing a keg of rum with them on a ship charged with transporting other types of cargo.[84] For the lone crewman, the decision allowed him to make some extra money. For Britain at large, it was pretty much the same thought process, as the empire derived a good share of its revenue from the external taxes imposed by these trade laws.

When Parliament passed new revenue laws in the mid-1760s, including the Sugar Act and the Stamp Act, it viewed them as extensions of maritime trade, and in keeping with this view, it granted jurisdiction over violations of these laws to "any court of admiralty, in the respective colony or plantation where the offence shall be committed, or [any] court of vice admiralty appointed or to be appointed."[85] This meant that if a local Pennsylvania publisher

---

83 Stephen Hopkins, *The Rights of Colonies Examined* (Providence, RI, 1764).
84 Neil R. Stout, *The Royal Navy in America: 1760-1775* (Annapolis, MD: Naval Institute Press, 1973), 37.
85 Duties in American Colonies for Defending, Protecting and Securing the Same Act, 1765, 5 Geo. 3, c. 12.

printed and sold a newspaper to residents in a landlocked region of the colony, and failed to use paper bearing the official revenue stamp, the violation could now be tried in a maritime court, in the same docket as high-seas smugglers and foreign pirates. To handle the increase in new cases, the Crown enhanced the number of these courts, including a new Vice-Admiralty Court for All America in Halifax, Nova Scotia.

Unlike local and provincial courts, the dictates of admiralty courts were overseen by judges alone, with no input from a jury of peers. The demands of evidence, likewise, were lower in such courts, and the burden of proof rested with the defendant instead of with the government. George Mason believed that "the ancient trial by jury is preferable to any other" in all cases involving property, of which trade crimes were a subset.[86] The more emotional John Adams called the extension of power in the maritime courts

> the most grievous innovation of all.... In these courts, one judge presides alone! No juries have any concern there! The law and the fact are both to be decided by the same single judge, whose commission is only during pleasure, and with whom, as we are told, the most mischievous of all customs has become established, that of taking commissions on all condemnations; so that he is under a pecuniary temptation always against the subject.[87]

---

86 "Wednesday, June 12, 1776," in *The Proceedings of the Convention of Delegates, Held at the Capitol, in the City of Williamsburg, in the Colony of Virginia, on Monday the 6th of May, 1776* (1776; Richmond, VA: Ritchie, TrueHeart & Duval, 1816), 42-45.

87 John Adams et. al, "Instructions Adopted by the Braintree Town Meeting," September 24, 1765, in *Papers of John Adams*, vol. 1, *September 1755 to October 1773*, ed. Robert J. Taylor (Cambridge, MA: Harvard University Press, 1977), 1:137-140.

Parliament rolled back some of its taxes in the colonies, including a repeal of the Stamp Act in 1766, just a year after its initial passage. But the power of the Courts of Admiralty remained, with their juryless proceedings and their "manifest tendency to subvert the rights and liberties of the colonists."[88] As with the previous grievance, it wasn't just about the money, but about personal liberty, since "if once it were left in the power of any the highest magistrate to imprison arbitrarily whomever he or his officers thought proper...there would soon be an end of all other rights and immunities."[89]

Grievance 19
For Transporting us beyond Seas to be Tried for Pretended Offences

In April 1772, Parliament passed "An Act for the better securing and preserving his Majesty's Dock Yards, Magazines, Ships, Ammunition, and Stores."[90] One's first thought on hearing of such a law in the context of American history is that it was a response to significant dockyard violence or destruction. But the Boston Tea Party had yet to occur. Instead, the law seems to have been driven in part by the desire for political support from dockworkers and members of the navy. In 1771, almost a year before the new law passed, the admiralty asked for 25,000 new civilian workers to guard docks, providing steady jobs for thousands of common laborers, and freeing marines from mundane land-based tasks so

---

88 "Declaration of Rights 1765," in *National Documents: State Papers So Arranged as to Illustrate the Growth of our Country from 1606 to the Present Day*, (New York: Unit Book Publishing Co., 1906) 34-36.
89 William Blackstone, *Commentaries on the Laws of England*, 1:131.
90 Dockyards, etc. Protection Act, 1772, 12 Geo. 3, c. 24.

that they could perform their stated (and revenue-generating) duties on the seas.[91]

However focused on jobs the act may have been, it included language that allowed violators of the law to be "indicted and tried…in any shire or county within this realm…as his Majesty, his heirs, or successors, may deem most expedient for bringing such offender to justice." The law, as understood by the colonists, allowed "any Person suspected, or pretended to be suspected" of destroying naval property to be

> hurried to Great Britain to take his Trial in any County the King or his Successors shall please to direct; where, innocent or guilty, he is in great danger of being condemned, and, whether condemned or acquitted, he will probably be ruined by the Expense attending the Trial, and his long Absence from his Family and Business.[92]

Such hurrying to the King's Bench was viewed as a violation of the rights of British citizens living in America, since "the respective colonies are entitled to the common law of England, and more especially to the great and inestimable privilege of being tried by their peers of the vicinage, according to the course of that law."[93] The law was, in its way, a self-fulfilling prophecy. In June 1772, just months after passage of the act (though word of the new rules had not yet reached America), residents of Rhode Island attacked and destroyed the British schooner *Gaspee*, and therefore fell under the jurisdiction of any British court empowered to adjudicate the

---

91 Nicholas Tracy, *Navies, Deterrence, and American Independence: Britain and Seapower in the 1760s and 1770s* (Vancouver: University of British Columbia Press, 1988), 36.
92 Samuel Adams, "The Rights of the Colonists […]," called the *Boston Pamphlet*. See Indictment #10.
93 "Resolutions Declaring the Rights and Grievances of the Colonies," in *American Archives, Fourth Series*.

law, although in fact the perpetrators were charged with the greater crime of treason.

GRIEVANCE 20
FOR ABOLISHING THE FREE SYSTEM OF ENGLISH LAWS IN A NEIGHBOURING PROVINCE, ESTABLISHING THEREIN AN ARBITRARY GOVERNMENT, AND ENLARGING ITS BOUNDARIES SO AS TO RENDER IT AT ONCE AN EXAMPLE AND FIT INSTRUMENT FOR INTRODUCING THE SAME ABSOLUTE RULE INTO THESE COLONIES:

As part of the spoils from its victory in the Seven Years' War, England acquired most of France's possessions in the Western Hemisphere, including its lands in Canada, and the so-called Indian Reserve, which together stretched south toward the Gulf of Mexico. In October 1763, King George III issued a royal proclamation[94] that all of the Indian lands between the Appalachian Mountains and the Mississippi River were temporarily, "for the present, and until Our further Pleasure be known," off limits to colonial settlers, even those who had moved into the area already. Any land grants issued previously in this region were summarily invalidated. It was a vexing move for colonies looking to push their boundaries westward. Still, there was hope that once the royal "Pleasure be known," those areas would be opened once again to purchase and settlement.

By now it should be obvious that things didn't pan out in favor of the colonies. Instead, Parliament passed the Quebec Act in 1774, which turned a major portion of those lands—covering modern-day Ontario, Ohio, Indiana, Illinois, Michigan, Wisconsin, and northeast Minnesota—into an enhanced and politically

---
94 "By the King, a Proclamation," *London Gazette*, October 8, 1763.

divergent Quebec.[95] Not only did it make permanent the "for the present" exclusion on American settlements in the area (including portions of the Ohio River valley that New York, Pennsylvania, and Virginia presumed to be part of their charter grants[96]), it also set up a government that was everything the patriots most feared from a despotic Britain. Most vexing: no elected assembly. Instead, the royal governor would select his own legislative council, and Crown officials would also install judges at all levels, except those handling civil suits. "The legislative, executive and judging powers," concluded the First Continental Congress, "are all moved by the nods of a Minister."[97]

Although some colonists were repulsed at seeing government positions in Quebec open to practicing Roman Catholics—"the introduction of popery, that grand fountain of arbitrary power"[98]—the official response from America was one of fraternity and vigilance on behalf of the Canadians. In an open letter penned to the Quebecois people, Congress welcomed delegates from the enlarged province to join the upcoming Second Continental Congress in May 1775. That document also warned of the certain tyranny embedded in Quebec's enabling legislation, specifically its absence of five vital freedoms: representative government, trial by jury, *habeas corpus*, land ownership, and freedom of the press. By uniting in purpose with the American colonies, Canada could

---

95 British North America (Quebec) Act, 1774, 14 Geo. 3, c. 83.
96 Gordon Wood, *The American Revolution* (New York: Random House, 2002).
97 "Address to the Inhabitants of the Province of Quebec," in *American Archives, Fourth Series*, 1:930-934.
98 Town of Mansfield Official Records, "Mansfield Declaration of Freedom," *Local History: Mansfield, CT*, http://mansfieldpubliclibraryct.org/history/items/show/294.

strive for "the perfect security of the natural and civil rights" of its citizens.[99]

Grievance 21
For taking away our Charters, abolishing our most valuable Laws, and altering fundamentally the Forms of our Governments:

Thomas Hutchinson, the royal governor of Massachusetts during some of that province's most trying moments, was no fan of the *Declaration of Independence*. In October 1776, he penned a letter to Lord North, providing a point-by-point rebuttal of the *Declaration*'s content. He found little to agree with in the document, stating for the record that the list of grievances was without merit—except for this one. "There has been no Colony Charter altered," he said, "except that of Massachusetts Bay."[100] And altered it was, significantly modified by Parliament through the Massachusetts Government Act, in March 1774.

By that act, England tried to clamp down on the rebellious colony by, among other things, altering the way that it chose its leaders. Massachusetts had an unusual provision in its 1691 charter that allowed the legislature to select, on an annual basis, the governor's executive council. But Lord North believed that this colonial freedom, far from "promoting of the internal welfare, peace, and good government of the said province," instead

> had the most manifest tendency to obstruct, and, in great measure, defeat, the execution of the laws…, to weaken the attachment of his Majesty's well-disposed subjects…, and to encourage the ill-disposed among

---

99 "Address to the Inhabitants of the Province of Quebec," in *American Archives, Fourth Series*.
100 Thomas Hutchinson, *Strictures upon the Declaration of the Congress at Philadelphia in a Letter to a Noble Lord*.

them to proceed even to acts of direct resistance to, and defiance of, his Majesty's authority.[101]

The new law also gave the royal governor the power "to nominate and appoint...and also to remove, without the consent of the council," pretty much every judge, sheriff, and official of any importance within the colony. Towns were also forbidden to call together their own councils "without the leave of the governor," since such meetings had been the breeding ground for "many dangerous and unwarrantable resolves." Given Governor Hutchinson's response to the *Declaration*, his disinclination to approve any but the most mundane agendas is not surprising. Taken as a whole, these changes essentially gutted a core feature of Massachusetts's charter, that of self-governance.

Edmund Burke, one of America's most ardent supporters within Parliament, understood how an attack on a colonial charter would bring about a worsening of relations across the Atlantic. "What can the Americans believe," he declared before the House of Commons, "but that England wishes to despoil them of all liberty, of all franchises; and by the destruction of their charters to reduce them to a state of the most abject slavery?"[102] It did not take long for Burke's prescience to prove itself, since as one of the Intolerable Acts, the Massachusetts Government Act became one of the strongest activators in the move toward war between America and England.

GRIEVANCE 22
FOR SUSPENDING OUR OWN LEGISLATURES, AND DE-

---

101 Massachusetts Government Act, 1774, 14 Geo. 3, c. 45.
102 Excerpts from Burke's speech. See Benson J. Lossing, *Pictorial Field-Book of the Revolution* (New York: Harper & Brothers, 1850), 1:505.

CLARING THEMSELVES INVESTED WITH POWER TO LEGISLATE FOR US IN ALL CASES WHATSOEVER.

As Jefferson closes out the section on Parliament's many sins, he links their actions directly to those of King George III. The "suspending our own Legislatures" charge documented here tracks closely with the "dissolved Representative Houses repeatedly" accusation from grievance 5. While some might quibble over the esoteric differences between "suspending" and "dissolved," the effect on the colonies was comparable, that of having a government that usurped the consent of the governed. The key difference between the two grievances is the identity of the offending actor: the king in the former, Parliament in the latter.

Another repeated theme from earlier in the document is the "in all cases whatsoever" clause. This is a quote from the Declaratory Act of 1766, tied closely to the start of the Parliament-focused section, in grievance 13. When the British legislature repealed the 1765 Stamp Act, it also tacked on the Declaratory Act as a way of saying, "We heard your complaints about taxation and have opted to retreat for now. But don't start falling in love with your American ideas of self-governance. We in Parliament are the governance, and if we so desire, we will legislate you however we want, 'in all cases whatsoever.'"

Despite that general link to the king's offenses, Jefferson also had in mind a specific legislative suspension, which he fleshed out in his earlier *Summary View*: the New York Restraining Act of 1767.[103] This was Parliament's rebuke against New York for its refusal to fully implement the Quartering Act. "One free and independent legislature," he wrote in 1774, "hereby takes upon itself to suspend the powers of another, free and independent as itself;

---
103 Rebellion in America Act, 1767, 7 Geo. 3, c. 59. Also called the "New York Restraining Act."

thus exhibiting a phenomenon unknown in nature, the creator and creature of its own power."[104] He might also have had in mind the more recent suspension of the Virginia House of Burgesses in 1774, by Lord Dunmore, then the royal governor of that colony. This act led the Virginia gentry to start their own House of Burgesses, and run it as if it were the real thing.

GRIEVANCE 23
HE HAS ABDICATED GOVERNMENT HERE, BY DECLARING US OUT OF HIS PROTECTION AND WAGING WAR AGAINST US.

The final block of five grievances addresses the active war between Britain and America, the cause of which, in the *Declaration*'s view, stems directly from the actions of the present King of England. In this, the first of those charges, George III is tied to two former kings whose misdeeds against Great Britain would have been well understood by all citizens.[105] The accusation that George had "abdicated Government here" parallels a similar complaint against James II, the last Roman Catholic king of England, who was deposed and subsequently fled to France during the Glorious Revolution of 1688.[106]

A generation earlier, the Rump House of Commons charged James's father, Charles I, with "waging war" against his own countrymen, and declared him "guilty of all the treasons, murders, rapines, burnings, spoils, desolations, damage, and mischief to this nation," a litany of transgressions not unlike those that Jefferson

---

104 Thomas Jefferson, *A Summary View of the Rights of British America*.
105 Stephen Lucas discusses the link between these last war-centric grievances and the two earlier kings of England. See Stephen Lucas, "Justifying America: The Declaration of Independence as a Rhetorical Document," 103.
106 In the 1689 English Bill of Rights, Parliament stated that James II had "abdicated the government" through his escape to the continent. See Bill of Rights, 1689, 1 W. & M. st. 2, c. 2.

applies to King George, though without the subsequent death sentence carried out against Charles.[107]

Beyond the insider terminology linking the current king to tyrannical monarchs of the past, Jefferson's core issue here is a speech by George III in October 1775, and a subsequent act of Parliament two months later, which together effectively threw the "thirteen colonies out of the royal protection, [leveled] all distinctions, and [made] us independent in spite of our supplications and entreaties."[108] In the speech, His Royal Highness announced the redirection of more troops to America's shores, so that "the unhappy and deluded multitude, against whom this force will be directed, shall become sensible of their error," after which "I shall be ready to receive the misled with tenderness and mercy."[109] Instead of employing the king's armies to protect his colonies against foreign aggressors, their armaments were to be turned against his own citizens.

The Prohibitory Act[110] that Parliament passed in December of that same year instituted a full naval blockade against the colonies, so that "all manner of trade and commerce is and shall be prohib-

---

107 For the act that created the court that would try Charles I, see "An Act of the Commons of England Assembled in Parliament, for Erecting of a High Court of Justice, for the Trying and Judging of Charles Stuart, King of England," January 1649, in *Acts and Ordinances of the Interregnum, 1642-1660*, 1253-1255. The list of crimes comes from the January 27, 1649 sentence of the High Court of Justice upon King Charles. See John Rushworth, *Historical Collections of Private Passages of State* (London: D Brown, 1721), 7:1418-1420.

108 From John Adams to Horatio Gates, Philadelphia, March 23, 1776, in *Papers of John Adams*, vol. 4, *February to August 1776*, 58-60.

109 King George III, "His Majesty's most gracious speech to both houses of Parliament, on Friday, October 27, 1775," in Library of Congress Printed Ephemera Collection, folio 108, folder 38, https://www.loc.gov/item/rbpe.10803800/.

110 Revolted Colonies, America Act, 1776, 16 Geo. 3, c. 5. Also called the "Prohibitory Act."

ited…and that all ships and vessels…together with their cargoes… found trading in any port or place of the said colonies, or going to trade, or coming from trading, in any such port or place, shall become forfeited to his Majesty." This confiscation of ships and goods could be effected without a court trial, and applied to all vessels dealing with the Americans, whether from the dominions or another nation. Far from protecting British citizens and their rights, the act put the goods, livelihood, and even the lives of those citizens outside of the Crown's protection.

GRIEVANCE 24
HE HAS PLUNDERED OUR SEAS, RAVAGED OUR COASTS, BURNT OUR TOWNS, AND DESTROYED THE LIVES OF OUR PEOPLE.

Formal hostilities between the American colonies and Great Britain began on April 19, 1775, with battles at Lexington and Concord, in Massachusetts. Initial British movements focused on Boston and the surrounding region, but the other provinces felt the impact as well, both in requests for martial support from General Washington, and from material resource procurements by British and American forces. The addition of the trade blockade in late 1775 brought a new level of involvement to some of the more distant colonies, including those whose seaport towns depended on the now outlawed international imports and exports. But the expanded theater was not just an American perspective; the British viewed all thirteen colonies as rebellious, and directed their rebukes, their laws, and their troops accordingly. As such, the Redcoats were not opposed to crushing colonial defiance, even if that meant destroying entire towns.

Consider the attack on the port town of Falmouth, now a part of Maine, but which at that time (like the rest of Maine) was incorporated into the Massachusetts Bay Colony. The destruction occurred on October 8, 1775, but the triggering incident took place four months earlier, and 180 miles east. Soon after the war began, General Thomas Gage, the British military commander overseeing the battles in Boston and beyond, sought out lumber and other supplies from Tory business leaders in Machias and other towns in eastern Maine, about 300 miles from Boston. He and Admiral Samuel Graves sent the British vessel *Margaretta* to ensure that the acquisition of lumber took place without incident. In mid-June 1775, about forty residents captured the ship, mortally wounding its captain. The capture of two more ships soon followed.

By October, the admiralty grew tired of these open attacks, so Graves sent Lieutenant Henry Mowat and a flotilla of four war ships to Maine "to chastize Marblehead, Salem, Newbury Port, Cape Anne Harbour, Portsmouth, Ipswich, Saco, Falmouth in Casco Bay, and particularly Machias" through retributive naval bombardment. Inclement weather around Machias pushed the fleet down to Falmouth, and after an overnight negotiated delay to allow the citizens to evacuate, the ships pounded the town, destroying 130 homes, the local Anglican church, public buildings, and a dozen ships moored in the harbor.[111]

As the war continued, "British Fleets and Armies have been and still are daily employed in destroying the People and committing the most horrid devastations on the Country."[112] By the time Congress ratified the *Declaration*, the British had lobbed munitions on several rogue port towns, all the way down to the Carolinas. This

---

111 Summary of the skirmishes in Maine as described in James S. Leamon, *Revolution Downeast: The War for American Independence in Maine* (Amherst, MA: University of Massachusetts Press, 1993), 67-73.

112 "The Struggle for Independence [Halifax Resolves]," in *North Carolina Manual*, 2008 ed. (Raleigh, NC: North Carolina Department of the Secretary of State, 2008), 73.

included Bristol, Rhode Island; Stonington, Connecticut; Norfolk, Virginia; and a failed assault on the southern city of Charleston, South Carolina, just days before the delegates in Philadelphia approved the resolution for independence.

Grievance 25
HE IS AT THIS TIME TRANSPORTING LARGE ARMIES OF FOREIGN MERCENARIES TO COMPLEAT THE WORKS OF DEATH, DESOLATION AND TYRANNY, ALREADY BEGUN WITH CIRCUMSTANCES OF CRUELTY & PERFIDY SCARCELY PARALLELED IN THE MOST BARBAROUS AGES, AND TOTALLY UNWORTHY THE HEAD OF A CIVILIZED NATION.

The obviousness of war meant that not only would the British need to fight the Americans, they would have to pay for it. The Seven Years' War had not been cheap—hence the taxes imposed on America—so why not find a less expensive supply of soldiers? Fortunately for Britain, several German princes were in the business of supplying such troops, and on desirable terms. Prince William, the head of the independent county of Hanau, near Frankfort, practically begged England to take his troops, putting them at King George's disposal for a negotiated price, but otherwise "without making the smallest condition."[113]

In debates before Parliament in February 1776, Lord North encouraged the use of such foreign soldiers, with the great object of "reducing America to a proper constitutional state of obedience." While Britain could send its own sons across the Atlantic, "men could be readier had, and upon much cheaper terms" by drawing from the population of continental serfs. His argument wasn't a slam dunk, and Lord Cavendish rose to reprobate the measure,

---

[113] Edward J. Lowell, *The Hessians and the Other German Auxiliaries of Great Britain in the Revolutionary War* (New York: Harper & Brothers, 1884), 7.

stating for the record that "Britain was to be disgraced in the eyes of all Europe" if it depended on Germans for its might. Fellow parliamentarian James Luttrell also worried about the loyalty of such troops, since 150,000 Germans had already found their way to the colonies.[114]

However, the present need was for manpower, and the Crown eventually negotiated with the heads of six separate European fiefdoms for their hired mercenaries: Frederick II, the Landgrave of Hesse-Cassel; William, his son, Count of Hesse-Hanau; Charles I, Duke of Brunswick; Frederick, Prince of Waldeck; Charles Alexander, Margrave of Anspach-Bayreuth; and Frederick Augustus, Prince of Anhalt-Zerbst.[115] Collectively, close to 30,000 German troops fell under the British command. More than a third of these never returned to Europe.

The first wave of German fighters didn't leave their homeland until late February 1776, arriving at Staten Island in mid-August. While the king was "at this time transporting large Armies of foreign Mercenaries" across the ocean, they would not touch American soil until more than a month after Congress voted for independence.

GRIEVANCE 26
HE HAS CONSTRAINED OUR FELLOW CITIZENS TAKEN CAPTIVE ON THE HIGH SEAS TO BEAR ARMS AGAINST THEIR COUNTRY, TO BECOME THE EXECUTIONERS OF THEIR FRIENDS AND BRETHREN, OR TO FALL THEMSELVES BY THEIR HANDS.

The Prohibitory Act mentioned back in grievance 23 included features that allowed not only British citizens, but anyone engaged in trade with the American colonies to be taken captive at sea. The

---
114 "February 29, 1776," *The Parliamentary Register* (London, 1802), 3:341-342.
115 Edward J. Lowell, *The Hessians and the Other German Auxiliaries [...]*, 3.

law enabled British vessels, upon capturing such a trade ship, to take not just the goods, but also "the masters, crews, and other persons" found on those ships, and put their names in the "books of his Majesty's said ships or vessels." Once documented, the captives could be impressed into "the service of his Majesty, to all intents and purposes, as if the said mariners and crews had entered themselves voluntarily to serve on board his Majesty's said ships and vessels."[116]

The law allowed British captains to omit some of the captured from the ships roles, provided that they be dropped off at a port back in England or "in any port in America not in rebellion." But for those kept on board, the expectation was obvious: They would be forced to fight on behalf of Britain, and against the American "defiance to the just and legal authority of the king and parliament of Great Britain." John Adams called it a "piratical Act," and understood it to be "a compleat Dismemberment of the British Empire."[117]

In response, the Continental Congress passed its own reciprocal Privateering Resolution, which authorized any American citizen or colony "to fit out armed vessels to cruize on the enemies of these United Colonies." If such ships were able to capture a vessel "belonging to any inhabitant or inhabitants of Great Britain," the captured ships and everything on them could be declared the "lawful prize" of the American vessel, and once the crew engaging in the capture had been adequately paid, any remaining value would be "for the use of the owner or owners, and the officers, marines, and mariners of such armed vessel."[118]

---

116 Revolted Colonies, America Act, 1776, 16 Geo. 3, c. 5.
117 From John Adams to Horatio Gates, Philadelphia, March 23, 1776.
118 Passed on March 23, 1776. See *Journals of the Continental Congress, 1774-1789*, 4:229-232.

In short, the Congress authorized Americans to plunder enemy ships. And the colonists were more than ready for the pirate life, such that by June 1776, Robert Morris was already reporting that "two New York Pilot Boats that were fitted out as Privateers from hence have taken three large Ships bound from Jamaica to London" carrying wine, foodstuffs, and "22000 hard Dollars."[119] American ships eventually captured or destroyed around 600 British ships.[120]

Grievance 27
He has excited domestic insurrections amongst us, and has endeavoured to bring on the inhabitants of our frontiers, the merciless Indian Savages, whose known rule of warfare, is an undistinguished destruction of all ages, sexes and conditions.

Guy Johnson, the Superintendent of Indian Affairs for America, took his job seriously, that of maintaining peaceful relations between the various North American tribes and the British citizens living on the western frontier lands of each colony. At a gathering in August 1774, the Six Nations had presented him with a "Great Old Covenant Chain Belt," representing the "chain of friendship between the English and the Six Nations." The natives even agreed to persuade another tribe, the Shawnee, not to make war on settlers in Virginia. For his part, Johnson assured the chiefs that "soon the king would right the wrongs inflicted upon his Indian allies by his wicked subjects and the Indian homeland would once more be undisturbed by rapacious intruders," a charge that at this time still

---

119 From Robert Morris to Silas Deane, June 5, 1776, in Connecticut Digital Archive, http://collections.ctdigitalarchive.org/islandora/object/40002:5222.
120 Edgar Stanton Maclay, *A History of American Privateers* (New York: D. Appleton and Co., 1899), viii.

focused on those who abused the relationship with the Indians, rather than on those abusing the king.[121]

By early 1775, the superintendent's outlook had changed, and he began to worry about the influence of the Americans, especially the New England missionaries sent into each tribe. He issued orders preventing the missionaries from visiting the tribes, and warned the natives to avoid white settlements, "since the Americans could not be trusted." At a gathering in Montreal in July, Johnson's associates regaled the tribes with "an Account of the Beginning of the Rebellion and undutifull as well as most ungratefull Behaviour of the Americans towards their Mother Country." Though the Six Nations had repeatedly stressed their neutrality, Johnson reminded them of their alliance with England, and soon after the natives were invited to metaphorically "feast on a Bostonian and drink his Blood." One chief informed American General Philip Schuyler, then in Albany, who sent a missive to the Congress detailing the event. While the Americans had been doing their own schmoozing with the local tribes, John Hancock was indignant upon hearing of Johnson's tactics: "We now have a full Proof that the Ministerial Servants have attempted to engage the Savages against Us."[122]

While Virginians along the frontier had to contend with native tribes, those who lived in the population centers to the east were concerned about slave uprisings, instituted by agents of the Crown.

---

121 Barbara Graymont, *The Iroquois in the American Revolution* (Syracuse, NY: Syracuse University Press, 1972), 50-53.
122 Barbara Graymont, *The Iroquois in the American Revolution*, 58-68. The December 14 letter from General Schuyler is mentioned in *Journals of the Continental Congress, 1774-1789*, 3:443. See the entry for December 22, 1775. For the letter itself, see From Philip Schuyler to the Continental Congress, December 14, 1775, in *Papers of the Continental Congress* (National Archives), no. 153, I, folio 362. For the quote from Hancock, see William L. Stone, *Life of Joseph Brant-Thayendanegea* (1838; repr., Albany, NY: Munsell, 1865), 1:112-13.

In mid-April 1775, the Virginia governor, Lord Dunmore, fearing a rebellion, ordered the supply of gunpowder held in the capital of Williamsburg to be removed to royal ships sitting in Chesapeake Bay. His concern was not without merit; just one day earlier (though the governor was not aware of it), the Revolutionary War began in Massachusetts, prompted in part by colonial control of gunpowder magazines.

The House of Burgesses insisted that the lack of gunpowder put the colony at risk, but the governor would not relent. When the crowds demanded the return of the military supply, Lord Dunmore threatened them, declaring that he would grant "Freedom to the Slaves, and lay the Town in Ashes," and warning them that he "could easily depopulate the whole Country."[123] The situation deteriorated significantly by the end of 1775, and in November he declared "all indented servants, Negroes, or others (appertaining to rebels) free," encouraging them to join the king's troops "for the more speedily reducing this colony to a proper sense of their duty to his Majesty's crown and dignity."[124]

REMOVED SECTION
ON THE ISSUE OF SLAVERY

Jefferson's original draft of the *Declaration* includes, at this point, a section addressing the issue of slavery. In the paragraph, he charges George III with a "cruel war against human nature itself" by "captivating & carrying [a distant people] into slavery in another hemisphere, or to incur miserable death in their transportation thither." Though there had been attempts within the colonies to restrict the

---

123 From House of Burgesses to Governor Dunmore, *Journals of the House of Burgesses of Virginia*, ed. John Pendleton Kennedy (Richmond, VA, 1905), 253-262.
124 "A Proclamation by his Excellency the Right Honorable John Earl of Dunmore," *Virginia Gazette (Dixon and Hunter)*, November 25, 1775.

slave trade, that "assemblage of horrors," Jefferson places blame for the failure on the king himself, who, "determined to keep open a market where *men* should be bought & sold, he has prostituted his negative for suppressing every legislative attempt to prohibit or to restrain this execrable commerce."

Jefferson and several of the signers were themselves slaveholders, yet he clearly identifies the practice as a violation of the "most sacred rights of life & liberty," although in the text, it is the king of England violating those rights, not the aggrieved Americans. Worse still, he denounces the king as violating not just human rights, but the law of God himself, since the king's acts of "piratical warfare" are "the opprobrium of *infidel* powers," unworthy of "the *Christian* king of Great Britain." And if that sin were not enough, the king compounds his own transgression by

> now exciting those very people to rise in arms among us, and to purchase that liberty of which *he* has deprived them, by murdering the people upon whom *he* also obtruded them; thus paying off former crimes committed against the *liberties* of one people, with crimes which he urges them to commit against the *lives* of another.

This block does not, of course, call for the elimination of slavery as an institution, nor does it explicitly demand that the king bring the buying and selling of human beings to an end. Rather, the passage exists to clarify, through yet one more example, how King George and his Parliament have illegally injected themselves into the political and legal affairs of the colonies. While the king may have "determined to keep open" slave markets, that clause exists primarily to support the main part of the sentence, in which the king "has prostituted his negative for suppressing every legislative attempt to prohibit" laws that restrict slavery. Slavery is bad;

overriding colonial legislatures, it seems, is worse. And while slavery is a violation of natural rights, the king's act of "exciting those very people to rise in arms" is the compounding aspect that makes it sufficiently relevant for inclusion in the grievance list.

Congress excised this entire block from the final document. As the framers did with the Constitution a decade later, the congressional delegates debating the merits of the *Declaration* opted to punt on the issue of slavery for the sake of continental unity. Additionally, had the section remained, it may have distracted from the main purpose of documenting grievances. While the twenty-seven line items seen so far stemmed from actions of the Crown and Parliament, the charge of violating human rights through slavery could be applied not only to those British bodies, but also to a segment of the American population and regional government institutions. The purpose of the entire list was to enumerate the sins of King George. Including a section that made the Americans appear as anything other than victims would have diluted the impact.

Repeated Injury by an Unfit Ruler
In every stage of these Oppressions We have Petitioned for Redress in the most humble terms: Our repeated Petitions have been answered only by repeated injury. A Prince whose character is thus marked by every act which may define a Tyrant, is unfit to be the ruler of a free people.

British citizens retained the right to petition their government and demand action on errant legislation. The 1689 English Bill of Rights could not have been clearer: "it is the right of the subjects to petition the king," and since the king's authority was overseen by Parliament, and by extension the citizenry, those citizens also had the right to petition the House of Commons and the House of Lords for redress of grievances. There was an expectation that "the equity and justice of a bill may be questioned, with perfect submission to the legislature."[125] And while the Americans balked at the idea that they owed any submission to Parliament, they were more than willing to address their complaints to the throne.[126]

The immediate complaints of the colonists began in earnest in 1765, soon after passage of the Stamp Act, with its dramatic increase in enforcement and management from afar. The Parliament brought to the colonies and plantations "many infringements and violations of the foregoing rights...since the last war, which demonstrate a system formed to enslave America."[127] While Parliament repeatedly and at times obnoxiously rebuffed the blunt appeals by American legislatures and pamphleteers, it is not true to say that repeated injury was the *only* response. That initial Stamp Act had most of its elements repealed just months after the protests began, and there were members of the House of Commons who were supportive of the American viewpoint.

Still, there were injuries, and they were not only repetitive, but incrementally harsh, moving from light taxation, to a military presence, to the removal of the king's protection over his remote dominions. This last action was, perhaps, the core frustration, that the king would behave not as a monarch, but as a tyrant. The Americans never wavered in their belief that Parliament had no authority over them, given their lack of representation in that body. But up until the Continental Congress approved the *Declaration*, George

---

125 James Otis, *The Rights of the British Colonies Asserted and Proved* (Boston & London: J. Almon, 1764).
126 Blackstone documented a right "appertaining to every individual, namely, the right of petitioning the king, or either house of parliament, for the redress of grievances." See William Blackstone, *Commentaries on the Laws of England*, 1:138-139.
127 "Resolutions Declaring the Rights and Grievances of the Colonies," in *American Archives, Fourth Series*.

III remained the king of all British citizens residing in the various colonies. When he withdrew his protection from those citizens, he abandoned his regal mandate to preserve and defend them. As one signer wrote, "Allegiance to the king and obedience to the parliament are founded on very different principles. The former is founded on protection: the latter, on representation."[128] When that protection was lost, so was the authority of the king over those he no longer protected.

Our British Brethren
NOR HAVE WE BEEN WANTING IN ATTENTIONS TO OUR BRITTISH BRETHREN. WE HAVE WARNED THEM FROM TIME TO TIME OF ATTEMPTS BY THEIR LEGISLATURE TO EXTEND AN UNWARRANTABLE JURISDICTION OVER US.

In October 1774, as the First Continental Congress drew to a close, the delegates approved a set of resolves and publications, including an *Address to the People of Great Britain*.[129] The document starts out well enough, reminding British "Friends and Fellow-Subjects" that they are a nation "[led] to greatness by the hand of Liberty, and possessed of all the Glory that heroism, munificence, and humanity can bestow." But things quickly turned dark from there. Whereas England should be "giving support to Freedom" in the American colonies, whose residents "are descended from the same common ancestors," it instead has become an "advocate for Slavery and Oppression," perhaps due to being "extremely negligent in the appointment of her Rulers."

---
128 James Wilson, "Considerations on the Nature and Extent of the Legislative Authority of the British Parliament," in *Collected Works of James Wilson* (1774; Indianapolis: Liberty Fund, 2007), 1:21-38.
129 "Address to the People of Great Britain," in *American Archives, Fourth Series*, 1:917-921.

The letter itemizes many of the same complaints found in the *Declaration*, including threats on trial by jury, the open violation of colonial charters, and the imposition of taxes on America without first obtaining direct or representative consent. Because the first Congress convened specifically to address the Intolerable Acts, those laws as passed by Parliament receive special condemnation, as does the authority of Parliament in general. "Why then are the Proprietors of the soil of America less lords of their property than you are of yours [in England]? Or why should they submit it to the disposal of your Parliament, or any other Parliament or Council in the world, not of their election?"

The individual colonies had issued similar missives to the British over the years. In April 1775, just a week after war broke out in Lexington and Concord, the Massachusetts Provincial Congress published an open letter to the inhabitants of Great Britain, "appealing to Heaven for the justice of our cause." The core of the letter, written by Joseph Warren, provided details on the recent battles between Massachusetts colonists and British regulars. But it quickly transformed into a rejection of Parliament and its unwarrantable acts, "measures highly incompatible with justice, but still pursued with a specious pretence of easing the nation of its burthens; measures which, if successful, must end in the ruin and slavery of Britain, as well as the persecuted American colonies."[130]

COLONIAL EMIGRATION
WE HAVE REMINDED THEM OF THE CIRCUMSTANCES OF OUR EMIGRATION AND SETTLEMENT HERE. WE HAVE APPEALED TO THEIR NATIVE JUSTICE AND MAGNANIMITY, AND WE HAVE CONJURED THEM BY THE TIES OF OUR COMMON KINDRED TO DISAVOW THESE

---

130 "Address of the Provincial Congress of Massachusetts to the Inhabitants of Great Britain," in *American Archives, Fourth Series*, 2:487.

USURPATIONS, WHICH, WOULD INEVITABLY INTERRUPT OUR CONNECTIONS AND CORRESPONDENCE.

The colonists had previously addressed the nature of the rights enjoyed by those who migrated from England to Great Britain, focusing on three overall aspects: (1) the general rights made available to all British citizens, regardless of the dominion in which they lived; (2) the specific rights granted to inhabitants of the various colonies and plantations, as documented in each jurisdiction's charter; and (3) the mutual benefit that England's relationship with America brought to both sides of the Atlantic.

Two years earlier, the First Continental Congress had stated clearly that "our ancestors, who first settled these colonies, were at the time of their emigration from the mother country, entitled to all the rights, liberties, and immunities of free and natural-born subjects, within the realm of England." Of course, there were the inherent rights that Jefferson discusses at the opening of the *Declaration*, rights "which nature has given to all men," including to those "departing from the country in which chance, not choice, has placed them."[131] But the earlier Congress also listed specific examples, such as the right to establish legislatures whose members derive their power from the governed; the extension of Common Law protections over all colonial citizens, including the protection of trial by jury; the freedom to assemble peaceably; and the right to petition the king.[132]

The authorization to enjoy these rights came not just from Nature's God, but also from the monarchs of England at the time each charter was granted. For instance, the right to settle New England came "by permission of King Charles I," who declared that

---

131 Thomas Jefferson, *A Summary View of the Rights of British America*.
132 Summarized from "Resolutions Declaring the Rights and Grievances of the Colonies," in *American Archives, Fourth Series*.

the new inhabitants of America would enjoy "all the freedom and liberty that the subjects in England enjoy," including the right to "make laws for their own government suitable to their circumstances, not repugnant to, but near as might be agreeable to the laws of England."[133] There were also provisos specific to each individual charter, some benefiting the colonists, some benefiting the Crown. The Massachusetts Bay charter of 1691, issued by William and Mary, guaranteed "a liberty of Conscience allowed in the Worshipp of God to all Christians (Except Papists)." That document also stipulated that "for the better provideing and furnishing of Masts for Our Royall Navy," all trees not already privately owned that were at least twenty-four inches in diameter belonged to the king.[134]

Beyond these legal benefits, America and Great Britain profited from the "harmonious intercourse" that open trade and mutual citizenship made possible "between the colonies and the kingdom from which they derived their origin." The tangible benefits were not limited to financial concerns, but also extended to security, as when the Americans fought alongside British regulars in the French and Indian War. This pan-oceanic brotherhood was "so extraordinary, as to excite astonishment," and was made possible because of those who traversed the Atlantic "at the expense of their blood, at the hazard of their fortunes, without the least charge to the country from which they removed, by unceasing labour, and an unconquerable spirit."[135]

---

133 Stephen Hopkins, *The Rights of Colonies Examined*.
134 "The Charter of the Province of the Massachusetts Bay in New England, 1691," *The Charters and General Laws of the Colony and Province of Massachusetts Bay* (Boston: T. B. Wait, 1814), 18-37.
135 Thomas Jefferson and John Dickinson, "Declaration of the Causes and Necessity of Taking Up Arms, July 6, 1775."

Through these prior communiques, the colonists hoped to rally their common British kindred to their defense, relying on their "native justice and magnanimity," concepts drawn from Aristotle's *Nicomachean Ethics*. Aristotle considered justice to be the greatest of virtues, and the complete embodiment of virtue, especially when it concerned human interactions in the political realm. Magnanimity refers to those who engage in virtuous behavior, and are justly honored as a result. What better way to act justly and receive honor than to aid your neighbors who have been treated with injustice.[136] That was the expectation of the Americans, who implored their British brethren to reason with their joint monarch and his wayward Parliament. While some in England took up America's cause for just treatment, it was not enough to maintain permanent ties between the colonies and their country of origin.

ENEMIES IN WAR, IN PEACE FRIENDS
THEY TOO HAVE BEEN DEAF TO THE VOICE OF JUSTICE AND OF CONSANGUINITY. WE MUST, THEREFORE, ACQUIESCE IN THE NECESSITY, WHICH DENOUNCES OUR SEPARATION, AND HOLD THEM, AS WE HOLD THE REST OF MANKIND, ENEMIES IN WAR, IN PEACE FRIENDS.

Montesquieu saw in civil societies two categories of laws: the *politic laws*, which determined the appropriate behavior of and between "the governors and the governed"; and the *civil laws*, which focused on interactions between members of society. These *positive laws* are social extensions of the natural law that applies to individuals in

---

136 Aristotle, *Nicomachean Ethics*. See Book 4 for magnanimity, and Book 5 for justice.

a state of nature, but that are now necessary with the advent of society and government.[137]

These laws apply to a nation's citizens. But above such constitutional arrangements, Montesquieu saw another law at work, which he named the *law of nations*. Just as individuals under a common government have codes that determine how they stand in relation to each other, the various nations also have rules at the global level, be they written or unwritten, that dictate how such states must interact and treat each other, especially when they have lost "the sense of their weakness" and entered into a state of war.

"The law of nations is naturally founded on this principle," wrote Montesquieu, "that different nations ought in time of peace to do one another all the good they can, and in time of war as little injury as possible, without prejudicing their real interests." This principle of being enemies in battle, but friends at all other times, played out with fair accuracy between the British and Americans, and Jefferson's version of this law of nations communicates the disappointment and regret of former friends now engaged in bitter war.

---

[137] Baron de Montesquieu (Charles Louis de Secondat), "Of Positive Laws," bk. 1, chap. 3, in *The Spirit of the Laws*, trans. in *The Complete Works of M. de Montesquieu*, vol. 1 of 4 (1748; London, 1777).

CHAPTER FOUR

Resolution of Independence

For modern Americans, the *Declaration of Independence* is a spiritual work of scripture, to be referenced as needed, or for those few immersed in the faith, to be consumed and praised. But if you examine its structure, you find that it most closely resembles governmental proclamations.

As an example, consider US Proclamation 5115, issued by President Ronald Reagan in October 1983, on the topic of school buses. After identifying the authority ("the President") and the title ("A Proclamation"), the text passes through introductory content ("More than twenty-two million young Americans use schoolbuses to get to school") and a list of justifications ("their safe transport deserves to be one of our highest priorities"). Eventually, a statement of actions appears ("Now, Therefore, I, Ronald Reagan, President of the United States of America, do hereby proclaim…"), translating the document's explanatory content into a firm resolve, either for the entity making the proclamation, or for the jurisdiction it represents. The proclamation ends with a signature block.

The *Declaration* follows this general layout. With the authorization, introduction, and justification portions now complete, it's time for action. This closing portion builds on the original resolution for independence from June 7, enhancing it to include not just the resolve, but the expected outcome of the act on the United

States and its people. In this way, the document was more than just a legal announcement of political intent. In the context of the ongoing war, the declaration of separation from England became a set of marching orders from a military command to those under its leadership. The announcement that America (or its constituent colonies) and Britain were now distinct states might have altered the legal understanding of the participants—at least on the American side—but the proclamation would have no impact unless the people acted to transform this template of liberty into reality.

The Declaration

WE, THEREFORE, THE REPRESENTATIVES OF THE UNITED STATES OF AMERICA, IN GENERAL CONGRESS, ASSEMBLED, APPEALING TO THE SUPREME JUDGE OF THE WORLD FOR THE RECTITUDE OF OUR INTENTIONS, DO, IN THE NAME, AND BY AUTHORITY OF THE GOOD PEOPLE OF THESE COLONIES, SOLEMNLY PUBLISH AND DECLARE,

Most of the ideas in this block—the unity of the colonies, the nature of the assembled Congress, the authority that brought them together, and the reliance on divine providence—made themselves known in previous entries. However, it is informative to consider a more enhanced edition of Jefferson's thoughts included in this lead-up to the actual resolution. Almost precisely one year earlier, Jefferson and Pennsylvania delegate John Dickinson co-authored *Declaration of the Causes and Necessity of Taking up Arms*, a publication of the Second Continental Congress that explained, as usual to a candid world, why the Americans had taken up arms against their British brethren. After explaining the specific circumstances and justifications for their aggressive decision, the document concludes with a joint appeal not only to the many nations of the earth, but to the Almighty.

Our cause is just. Our union is perfect. Our internal resources are great, and, if necessary, foreign assistance is undoubtedly attainable. We gratefully acknowledge, as signal instances of the Divine favour towards us, that his Providence would not permit us to be called into this severe controversy, until we were grown up to our present strength, had been previously exercised in warlike operation, and possessed of the means of defending ourselves. With hearts fortified with these animating reflections, we most solemnly, before God and the world, declare, that, exerting the utmost energy of those powers, which our beneficent Creator hath graciously bestowed upon us, the arms we have been compelled by our enemies to assume, we will, in defiance of every hazard, with unabating firmness and perseverence, employ for the preservation of our liberties; being with one mind resolved to die freemen rather than to live slaves.[1]

This clause also identifies clearly the "authority of the good People of these Colonies," recalling the natural rights that made the resolution for independence valid. The *Declaration*'s preamble invoked this authority, when it lamented the need for "one people to dissolve the political bands which have connected them with another." Here, the people appear once more, for it is not the individual colonies that are instigating this separation from England, but the collective residents of America. In fact, until the authority to withdraw from the British Empire was granted by the body politic, the Congress was powerless to take such an action.

---

1   Thomas Jefferson and John Dickinson, "Declaration of the Causes and Necessity of Taking Up Arms, July 6, 1775," in *Documents Illustrative of the Formation of the Union of the American States*, ed. Charles C. Tansill (Washington, DC: Government Printing Office, 1927), 10-17.

> **RESOLUTION OF INDEPENDENCE**
> THAT THESE UNITED COLONIES ARE, AND OF RIGHT OUGHT TO BE FREE AND INDEPENDENT STATES; THAT THEY ARE ABSOLVED FROM ALL ALLEGIANCE TO THE BRITISH CROWN, AND THAT ALL POLITICAL CONNECTION BETWEEN THEM AND THE STATE OF GREAT BRITAIN, IS AND OUGHT TO BE TOTALLY DISSOLVED;

The moment of treason has arrived. The content encountered thus far has been valuable and informative, not only as justification for colonial grievances, but also as a summation of some of the most important ideas coming out of the Enlightenment. The British might have disagreed with specific bullet points in Jefferson's writing—especially some of the negative comments concerning King George. But the text so far would not have surprised most readers, since nearly identical things had been issued previously from colonial legislatures, pamphleteers, and the First Continental Congress.

But this statement was new, not only it its intent, but also in its disloyalty to Great Britain, at least among the official public statements released from the general congress. Benjamin Franklin's quip, "We must, indeed, all hang together, or most assuredly we shall all hang separately," whether historical or apocryphal, rang true because of the association of the signers' names to this specific sentence in the larger document.

Thomas Jefferson did not write this particular clause. Instead, this "resolution of independence" was brought before the Congress on June 7, 1776, by Richard Henry Lee, a fellow Virginia delegate, acting on instructions from the Fifth Virginia Convention. Lee's Resolution, as it is now known, appears word-for-word in the *Declaration*, after having been formally approved as the legal separation statement just two days earlier, in a majority vote of Congress on July 2.² The utter repudiation of all political ties with England was certainly a cause for disquiet among the delegates. But perhaps Lee and Jefferson could find some courage through experience, since they both, as delegates and representatives of Virginia, had already committed the subversive act against their mother country. The Virginia gathering, back on May 15, had approved its own intent to separate from England, dissolving the royal government, and entering into a state of nature, as outlaws. Now they were bringing this same action, punishable by death, to the full collection of colonies.

The original version of this resolution, with some wording differences, was written by Edmund Randolph, and called on the delegates in the national congress "to declare the United Colonies free and independent States, absolved from all allegiance to, or dependence upon, the Crown or Parliament of Great Britain." By the time Lee presented it to Congress, it had been adjusted and embellished with language used in prior pronouncements. Most notable is the insertion of the phrase, "of right ought to be," which echoes similar language in the English Bill of Rights of 1689, the post-Glorious Revolution document in which William and Mary "did become, were, are and of right ought to be by the laws of this realm our sovereign liege lord and lady, king and queen of England...."³

FREE AND INDEPENDENT STATES
AND THAT AS FREE AND INDEPENDENT STATES, THEY HAVE FULL POWER TO LEVY WAR, CONCLUDE PEACE, CONTRACT ALLIANCES, ESTABLISH COMMERCE, AND

---

2   *Journals of the Continental Congress, 1774-1789*, June 7, 1776, 5:425. For the original proposal, see Lee Resolution, June 7, 1776, in *Papers of the Continental Congress* (National Archives), no. 23, folio 11.
3   Bill of Rights, 1689, 1 W. & M. st. 2, c. 2.

TO DO ALL OTHER ACTS AND THINGS WHICH INDEPENDENT STATES MAY OF RIGHT DO.

The second clause of the core resolution on independence, a seemingly simple passage covering the rights and activities of independent states, is perhaps one of the most difficult to analyze and understand. One key goal of this book has been to identify the writings and ideas that the Committee of Five employed in crafting the text of the document. But this block, while certainly based on concepts already understood by the delegates, is nonetheless a forward-looking statement that blurs the line between the states and the undefined nation under which they stood united.

Part of the problem has to do with the legal foundations for this new status as "Free and Independent States." At the moment when the *Declaration* was approved on July 4, only four colonies had promulgated replacement constitutions: New Hampshire, South Carolina, Virginia, and just two days earlier, New Jersey. In May, Rhode Island had declared that its royal charter would serve as the ongoing foundation of its government, sans the language binding it to Britain. But the other colonies delayed the passage of their own constitutions beyond their official separation from England, sometimes well into the nineteenth century.[4] Given that the legal status of all of the colonies was based on letters patent and royal grants from the British Crown, the legal import of those founding documents upon the colonies once the ties with Great Britain were severed was unclear at best and meaningless at worst.

---

4   Rhode Island didn't officially replace its royal charter with a true constitution until 1843. For a detailed look at the timeline of constitutional implementations, and the vague relationship between the states and the national government before the US Constitution went into effect, see Mark A. Graber, "State Constitutions and National Constitutions" (legal studies research paper 2016-30, University of Maryland Francis King Carey School of Law, 2016), https://ssrn.com/abstract=2817882.

The understanding became only slightly clearer when the Articles of Confederation went into effect in 1781. Eventually, the matter came before the court via *Camp v. Lockwood*, in 1788.[5] In that case, the court recognized the ambiguity of the authority between the states, the Congress, and Great Britain:

> When a resistance was made to the execution of the laws of Great Britain, and an actual war took place between us and them, we were not thirteen independent States, but Colonies and Provinces, belonging to, and a part of, a great Empire, comprehending both countries.... The first body that exercised anything like a sovereign authority, was the Congress of the then United Colonies, who superintended the whole, and, by the like common consent, were invested with such general powers as were necessary for the prosecution of the war. We afterwards divided ourselves into several distinct governments, by the name of States....

The *Declaration* advanced the several colonies to the level of Free and Independent States. But some of those states were nothing of the sort, since those entities, having turned their backs on the nation that provided them with their original colonial grants, no longer possessed functioning constitutions recognized by a candid world.

Aristotle lifted up the constitution as a key foundation for a civil society, a "form of organization of the inhabitants of a state." While a nation may be little more than a "collection of citizens," they engage in the actions of a state under the auspices of a constitution, and they carry out political duties under its direction.[6] Aristotle's constitution was not necessarily a printed document.

---

5 1 U.S. 393, 403 (Pa. 1788).
6 Aristotle, *Politics*, 3.1.1274b32, trans. H. Rackham, *Aristotle in 23 Volumes*, vol. 21 (Cambridge, MA, Harvard University Press, 1944).

But because the colonists where attempting to justify their right to exist apart from Britain, claiming that their charter from this point forward would simply be an expression of their Aristotelian soul would not prove convincing.

Great Britain granted authority to the colonies through charters and grants. The colonies granted authority to the Congress through legislative acts that sent delegates to the convention. When some royal governors abandoned their offices, abdicating their authority and leaving those colonies with "no government sufficient to the exigencies of their affairs," Congress recommended (which could be interpreted as granting permission) that those colonies "adopt such government as shall, in the opinion of the representatives of the people, best conduce to the happiness and safety of their constituents in particular, and America in general."[7]

This progression of authority back onto the colonies from Congress seems somewhat circular. But Jefferson, if he thought of this process at all, may have looked past it to the rights of the people themselves. For when those colonies that had not yet crafted replacement constitutions aborted their charters under Congress's general claim of independence, those bodies reverted back to their original state, that is, to the Lockean State of Nature. In this condition, the people had the right to reconstitute government as would "best conduce to the happiness and safety of their constituents." They would also benefit from the ongoing pseudo-sovereign existence of the Congress itself, which offered the cover of authority and respectability, especially since the states had for the most part delegated to Congress those powers that comprised international affairs, including the execution of the Revolutionary War.

The specific national rights documented in this block—levying war, concluding peace, contracting alliances, and establishing com-

---

7 *Journals of the Continental Congress, 1774-1789*, May 10, 1776, 4:342.

merce—were pillars of Britain's economic might at the tail end of its embrace of mercantilism. One of the dominant monetary theories in Europe from the sixteenth through eighteenth centuries, mercantilism sought to advance the power of the state by controlling local and global finance through the manipulation of raw materials and finished goods, while simultaneously disrupting or denying similar opportunities to other nations. War, peace, and advantageous alliances were essential tools in building the British Empire, and this willingness to do whatever it took to achieve economic might helped create the initial rift between England and its American colonies.

In *England's Treasure by Foreign Trade*, published posthumously in 1664, Thomas Mun defined and defended the constructs of mercantilism, and looked forward to England's glory under such a system.

> For what greater glory and advantage can any powerful Nation have, than to be thus richly and naturally possessed of all thing needful for Food, Rayment, War, and Peace, not onely for its own plentiful use, but also to supply the wants of other Nations, in such a measure, that much money may be thereby gotten yearly, to make the happiness compleat.[8]

The right to control war, peace, alliances, and commerce, at least to the extent that such things can be controlled, enables a nation to direct its destiny, and interact on the world stage with the other states already managing their own set of parallel rights.

APPEAL TO DIVINE PROVIDENCE
AND FOR THE SUPPORT OF THIS DECLARATION, WITH

---

[8] Thomas Mun, *England's Treasure by Forraign Trade* (1664; repr., New York: MacMillan Co., 1895), 98.

A FIRM RELIANCE ON THE PROTECTION OF DIVINE PROVIDENCE,

The religious terminology in Jefferson's original draft of the *Declaration* ended at "Nature's God." The full Congress, meeting together to hammer out the document's final language, inserted this reference to the divine Providence to pique "the ears of Reformed Americans, including Congregationalists, Presbyterians, Dutch and German Reformed, who collectively made up the largest religious constituency in the colonies in 1776, and a sizable political constituency."[9]

Deists in Jefferson's era did use Providence as a euphemism for their Creator, but creative agency implies a certain level of interest and ongoing activity on the part of that eternal being. It's a strange perspective for adherents of the Enlightenment who perceived the Supreme Being as an instrumental force in bringing the universe into existence and establishing its laws, but who was more standoffish when it came to further involvement. America in the late eighteenth century was already pluralistic, it seems, a mix of Anglicans, Baptists, Catholics, Deists, and an entire alphabet of other sects, some of whom placed a premium on the role of God in the regular affairs of men.

John Witherspoon, a signer from New Jersey and appointed as chaplain of the Congress by John Hancock, emphasized the role of Providence over the affairs of men, especially when afflicted by the unjust: "There is no part of divine providence in which a greater beauty and majesty appears, then when the Almighty Ruler turns the counsels of wicked men into confusion, and makes them militate against themselves." In this light, any victory, even a military

---

9   Jeffrey Morrison, "Political Theology in the Declaration of Independence," (lecture, James Madison Program in American Ideals and Institutions, Princeton University, April 5-7, 2002).

one, was seen as evidence of God's protection, since "the fury and injustice of oppressors shall bring in a tribute of praise to thee…; the countenance and support thou wilt give to thine own people shall be gloriously illustrated; thou shalt set the bounds which the boldest cannot pass."[10]

Witherspoon's words echo the thoughts of his fellow Reformed colleague, the late Jonathan Edwards, whose revivalist preaching helped extend the First Great Awakening throughout New England. God, in Edwards's parlance, was the "Supreme Judge of the World," and by right could direct the world and its inhabitants as he saw fit, especially when he "suffers so much injustice to take place in the world." Wicked deeds inflicted by individuals on others are abundant, but there are also

> many public wrongs, wrongs done by men acting in a public character, and wrongs which affect nations, kingdoms, and other public bodies of men.... Now it seems a mystery that these things are tolerated, when he that is rightfully the Supreme Judge and Governor of the world is perfectly just. But at the final judgment all these wrongs shall be adjudged, as well as those of a more private nature.[11]

Edwards spoke of the final judgment, when Christ himself would both judge and redeem. But if a temporal subset of that justice and redemption were to take place in the American colonies in the 1770s, who were the patriots to argue?

---

10 John Witherspoon, "The Dominion of Providence over the Passions of Men," in *Political Sermons of the American Founding Era: 1730-1805* (Indianapolis: Liberty Fund, 1998), 1:530-558.

11 Jonathan Edwards, "The Final Judgment," in *The Works of Jonathan Edwards*, ed. Anthony Uyl (London: John Childs and Son, 1834), 2:190-201.

MUTUAL PLEDGE
WE MUTUALLY PLEDGE TO EACH OTHER OUR LIVES, OUR FORTUNES AND OUR SACRED HONOR.

The pledge of the honor, the fortune, and even the life of each signer was a common emphatic flourish in declaratory statements of this era. Some were as compact as the version seen here; the First Continental Congress introduced the planks of its Continental Association with a commitment to work "under the sacred ties of virtue, honor and love of our country."[12] Other documents offered expanded claims of honor, further beating the ideas into the heads of readers or hearers through an increase in words.

Richard Henry Lee, the mover of the Resolution for Independence, tried his own hand at this sort of enhanced honor statement ten years earlier. In his *Westmoreland Resolutions*, before the rejections of the Stamp Act policies, before the confirmation of British citizenship, even before the pledge to obey "our lawful Sovereign, George the Third," he and his fellow northeastern Virginia residents did "bind ourselves to each other, to God, and to our country, by the firmest ties that religion and virtue can frame, most sacredly and punctually to stand by and with our lives and fortunes, to support, maintain, and defend each other in the observance and execution of these following articles."[13]

The link between one's honor and the veracity or strength of a pledge had a long history of support in England, going at least as far back as the reign of James I, in the early seventeenth century. In 1620, a discussion took place in Parliament as to whether peers were obligated to submit lawsuits and protests *under oath* before the

---

12 *Journals of the Continental Congress, 1774-1789*, October 20, 1774, 1:75-81.
13 "Westmoreland Resolutions," in *Westmoreland County, Virginia: A Short Chapter and Bright Day in its History*, ed. T. R. B. Wright (Richmond, VA: Whittet & Shepperson, 1912), 42-47.

court and Crown, or if they could instead appeal to their own personal honors in such situations. "The Lords all answered, *una voce*, that they conceived protestation, upon honor, to bind more than oath did; as being the same before God and before the world; and, in regard to the trust given to their degree, a far greater charge."[14]

Ending the text on this note of honor also had a way of humanizing the document. The ideas conveyed in the *Declaration*—the equality of all men, the intrinsic rights of life and liberty, the identification of common man as the foundation of government—had an eternal quality that tended to put them out of the reach of mere mortals. Linking these truths to the sacred honors of individual humans brought at least a portion of the transcendence back down to earth. It also offered a valid segue into the document's signature block, where most of those who voted for independence, plus a few alternates shuffled in from each state, would have their honors—and their lives—tested by British resolve and Redcoat munitions.

---

14 *Cobbett's Parliamentary History of England*, ed. William Cobbett et. al. (London: R. Bagshaw, 1806), 1:1202-3.

CHAPTER FIVE

Signature Block

With so much acclamation going to Thomas Jefferson for the core text of the *Declaration of Independence*, it's sometimes easy to forget that he was just one cog—albeit a cog with quality wordsmithing skills—in an American independence machine. The participants in the Continental Congress comprised a Who's Who of liberty luminaries. Many of the delegates had been long-term members of the colonial legislatures that sent them to the Congress, legislatures that in some cases had been prorogued by governors under the direction of the Crown. Others had led their towns and colonies in the patriot cause, through participation in Committees of Correspondence or similar organizations.

Active members of Congress had penned some of the most influential liberty-minded pamphlets going back to the Stamp Act conflict two decades earlier. A brief look at some publications written by other signers will show that Jefferson was not alone in his efforts to push back Parliament and King George as they sought to exert increasing control over the colonies.

STEPHEN HOPKINS
DELEGATE FROM RHODE ISLAND

Stephen Hopkins was one of those early pamphleteers whose work helped provide philosophical guidance for Americans unhappy with the sudden tax responsibilities imposed on them by

Parliament. His 1764 work, *The Rights of Colonies Examined*, offered a critique of the Stamp Act that read like an abolitionist sermon, with its appeals to slavery from the opening line: "Liberty is the greatest blessing that men enjoy, and slavery the heaviest curse that human nature is capable of."[1]

Hopkins's core argument was a common one during the Stamp Act crisis, namely, that as British citizens, the colonists could only be taxed by Parliament if they first gave their consent to that body. Thanks to their retained British citizenship, the authority to impose taxes on Americans rested solely with those Americans or their representatives in the House of Commons, though the latter group was notable by its absence. Parliament's imposition of taxes without colonial consent was a form of tyranny, Hopkins claimed, since "those who are governed at the will of another, or of others, and whose property may be taken from them by taxes, or otherwise, without their own consent, and against their will, are in the miserable condition of slaves."

The charters granted to each colony made clear the British citizenship rights of each resident, something Hopkins and his fellow patriots repeatedly told their English brethren. But to strengthen his point, he goes beyond something as mundane as government dictates, daring to invoke the Apostle Paul himself. It's a bit odd coming from a Rhode Island delegate, with that colony's emphasis on religious freedom and the separation of state authority from ecclesiastical power. One might expect this argument from a Virginian, with that jurisdiction's inherent ties to the Church of England.

Still, Hopkins's reference to the author of the Pastoral Epistles would have been familiar to Americans of any province. Paul came out of Tarsus, in modern-day Turkey, and was a Roman citizen thanks to Pompey's capture of the Cilician region along Turkey's

---

1   Stephen Hopkins, *The Rights of Colonies Examined* (Providence, RI, 1764).

Mediterranean coast. That citizenship followed Paul wherever he traveled within the Empire, and he was not hesitant to declare his position anytime someone violated his citizenship rights. When a team of Roman soldiers prepared to have Paul flogged at the behest of the angry crowds, he demanded to know if it was "legal for you [a centurion] to flog a Roman citizen who hasn't even been found guilty?" When the soldier's superiors heard Paul's claim, "the commander himself was alarmed when he realized that he had put Paul, a Roman citizen, in chains."[2]

With this background, Hopkins reminds the reader that British citizens anywhere in the realm retain their rights, as was the case with Rome.

> The Roman colonies did not, like the Grecian, become separate states, governed by different laws, but always remained a part of the mother state; and all that were free of the colonies, were also free of Rome, and had right to an equal suffrage in making all laws, and appointing all officers for the government of the whole common-wealth. For the truth of this, we have the testimony of St. Paul, who though born at Tarsus, yet assures us he was born free of Rome.

After showing by numerous examples that "colonies in general, both ancient and modern have always enjoyed as much freedom as the mother state from which they went out," Hopkins asks the logical question: "Will anyone suppose the British colonies in America, are an exception to this general rule?"

The answer, of course, is that no such exception exists. The flogging that threatened Paul came about after an angry mob in Jerusalem demanded justice. Residents of Judea, though covered by the shadow of Rome, were not granted citizenship, since their in-

---

2   Acts 22:22-29 (New International Version).

clusion within the Empire came about by conquest, not birth. But Paul was born a citizen, and he did not argue for his rights with the non-citizen mobs, but with a citizen-centurion. For his rights could not be removed without cause by any other citizen of the realm.

This is the heart of Hopkins's argument, that Parliament has no authority over Americans because British citizens in England have no power to remove the rights of fellow British citizens in America.

> Indeed, it must be absurd to suppose, that the common people of Great Britain have a sovereign and absolute authority over their fellow-subjects in America, or even any sort of power whatsoever over them; but it will be still more absurd, to suppose they can give a power to their representatives, which they have not themselves. If the House of Commons do not receive this authority from their constituents, it will be difficult to tell by what means they obtained it, except it be vested in them by mere superiority and power.

CHARLES CARROLL OF CARROLLTON
Delegate from Maryland

Influential communications via the written word were not limited to formal pamphlets. A common means of political colonial discourse appeared in the form of letters to newspapers, often submitted under a Latin or English pen name. These weren't today's terse letters-to-the-editor, but instead appeared as long-form serial dissertations extending over several printed issues, sometimes in tandem with a pseudonymous opponent.

Charles Carroll of Carrollton, a delegate from Maryland and the lone Roman Catholic signer, was one such letter writer. A lawyer by training, his family's religious preferences prevented him from practicing law in Maryland. So instead, he went into business and became rich. Beginning in 1772, he engaged in a series of printed debates in the *Maryland Gazette* under the pen name "First Citizen." Daniel Dulany, a member of the governor's council for the colony and styling himself as "Antilon," took the opposing view. The topic: whether the colonists had the right to control their own taxation.[3]

The specific argument involved an attempt by the governor of Maryland to renew an expiring law *by proclamation* that imposed fees on the citizenry for various functions of government. At one level, it was a minor quibble, as the fees had already existed for decades, and even Carroll admitted that at least some of the fees were reasonable in their amounts. But the principle of citizen rights was at risk, and although Carroll might have been fine with some specific fees, he was not fine with the manner in which they were imposed.

The printed debates frequently veered off into the minutiae of fees paid to officers for their duties, and the role of royal proclamations, especially during wartime—the original fees were established in 1763, in the midst of the French and Indian War. Dulany argued that the fees were legal even outside the legislative process, since they were not actually demands on citizens for payment, but upper limits on suggested payments to officers for services rendered. That is, the law was supposed to limit extortion and fraud. But an earlier legislature had rejected that argument, and so did Carroll.

"It has, I hope, been proved already, that fees are taxes, and that the settlement of them by Proclamation is arbitrary, and illegal," responded Carroll after several published interactions with Antilon. And not just illegal, but a "disguised and dangerous attack on

---

3   Elihu S. Riley, *"First Citizen"—Charles Carroll of Carrollton, and "Antilon"— Daniel Dulany, Jr., 1773* (Baltimore: King Bros. State Printers, 1902), with a focus on pages 122-123. The debates were originally printed in the *Maryland Gazette* from January to July, 1773.

liberty." Maryland legislators had debated the fees, but were unable to reach consensus before the governor dismissed them. "The proclamation came out a few days after the prorogation of the assembly.... The governor was therefore advised [by the Crown] to issue the proclamation for the settlement of fees, adopting the very rates of the late regulation objected to by your delegates, as unjust, and oppressive in several instances."

This act by the executive—bringing the legislative power under his control—was, for Carroll, a clear violation of the rights of Maryland citizens.

> Our constitution is founded on jealousy, and suspicion; its true spirit, and full vigour cannot be preserved without the most watchful care, and strictest vigilance of the representatives over the conduct of administration. This doctrine is not mine, it has been advanced, and demonstrated by the best constitutional writers.... The pursuits of government in the enlargements of its powers, and its encroachments on liberty, are steady, patient, uniform, and gradual; if checked by a well concerted opposition at one time, and laid aside, they will be again renewed by some succeeding minister, at a more favourable juncture.

RICHARD STOCKTON
DELEGATE FROM NEW JERSEY

While writers such as Charles Carroll could be blunt, or at times even belligerent, toward the loyalist members of society, others made a concerted effort find a common understanding with those who adhered to the official British position. One delegate from New Jersey, Richard Stockton, even went so far as to address King George directly in hopes of achieving long-term reconciliation between Great Britain and the American colonies.

His *Expedient for the Settlement of the American Disputes*, sent to His Majesty at the end of 1774, was terse even by the standards of the *Declaration of Independence*.[4] After acknowledging the very real drama consuming British citizens on both sides of the Atlantic to the point of violent war, Stockton presented his three-pronged approach.

The first item proposed a pan-Atlantic congress:

> That a royal Instruction be immediately obtained, and sent over to the several Governors of the North American Colonies, requiring them forthwith to recommend it to their several Assemblies to pass, and to give their own assent to an Act which may be passed by the Legislatures of the several Provinces, empowering certain Commissioners therein to be named, to repair to England; with power to confer with his Majesty's Ministers or with Commissioners to be appointed by Act of Parliament, respecting the grand points in dispute between Great Britain and America; and finally to determine thereupon.

Jefferson's flowing prose this is not. The subsequent two suggestions—that the governance between Parliament and the colonies be clarified or altered, and that the Boston Port Act be suspended—are equally dry, and yet they were bold, written with the desperate hope that reconciliation could be obtained. Drafted four months before the international conflict began at Lexington and Concord, Stockton could easily predict the future that would come quickly if tempers on both sides were not appeased. "Some expedient must be immediately fallen upon, or we shall be involved

---

[4] Richard Stockton, "An Expedient for the Settlement of the American Disputes," repr. in *The Historical Magazine*, ser. 2, vol. 4 (November 1868): 228-229.

in a civil war the most obstinate awful and tremendous that perhaps ever occurred since the Creation of the world."

JOSEPH HEWES
DELEGATE FROM NORTH CAROLINA

Some of the ideas generated by signers of the *Declaration* found their way into other official statements penned by the Congress. Such was the case with Joseph Hewes from North Carolina, who had been sent as a delegate to both the First and Second Continental Congresses. During the first gathering, he took part in a committee charged with documenting the rights of the Americans, and how Parliament had violated those rights.

The outcome of that committee effort was *The Declaration and Resolves of the First Continental Congress*, a set of nearly a dozen affirmations, mostly unanimous, that stated for the record those rights and violations.[5] There are some elements that have parallels in the *Declaration* from the subsequent congress, such as the clear assertion that by the authority of each colonial charter, British citizens in America "are entitled to life, liberty, and property, and they have never ceded to any sovereign power whatever a right to dispose of either without their consent."

As faithful colonists, loyal to the King of England, "they are entitled to the benefit of such of the English statutes, as existed at the time of their colonization," and "have a right peaceably to assemble, consider of their grievances, and petition the king." Perhaps such ideas would have been approved by moderate observers in Great Britain. But then there were the upstart claims that colonial legislatures could overrule the dictates of the Crown and

---

5   "Resolutions Declaring the Rights and Grievances of the Colonies," in *American Archives, Fourth Series*, ed. M. St. Clair Clark and Peter Force (Washington, DC, 1837), 1:910-912.

Parliament: "Keeping a standing army in these colonies, in times of peace, without the consent of the legislature of that colony, in which such army is kept, is against law."

As a Quaker, albeit one of the few of that faith to accept eventually the necessity of a war with England, Hewes was naturally inclined to do whatever it took to reconcile with Great Britain. But that "whatever" did not include a casual disregard for the core rights granted to every citizen of the realm, and as became clear in the *Declaration*, to every citizen of the earth.

JAMES WILSON
DELEGATE FROM PENNSYLVANIA

The American cry of "no taxation without representation," confrontational as it sounded, typically referred to *internal taxes*, those demanded of individual British citizens based on the daily routines of life, such as taxes on newspapers (via the 1765 Stamp Act), land (property taxes), and voting (poll taxes). *External taxes*, the kind charged to merchants and shipping companies at the moment of product import, existed to regulate commerce, it was understood, and many of the colonists who objected to internal American tax changes by Parliament had no problem with that same body imposing new or increased external taxes. The list of rights that Joseph Hewes helped craft for the First Continental Congress stated this directly, when it assured British leaders that

> we cheerfully consent to the operation of such acts of the British parliament as are bona fide restrained to the regulation of our external commerce, for the purpose of securing the commercial advantages of the whole empire to the mother country, and the commercial benefit of its respective members.

James Wilson from Pennsylvania did not view the distinction between internal and external taxes as a valid dividing line for acts of Parliament. In his *Considerations on the Nature and Extent of the Legislative Authority of the British Parliament*, Wilson proposed that the lack of American representation in the House of Commons meant that any British tax laws imposed on the colonies were invalid.[6] The foundation of his argument invoked the standard Locke line that "all men are, by nature, equal and free: no one has a right to any authority over another without his consent," and also that "all power is derived from the people," ideas that by 1774 must have become tiresome in the ears of parliamentarians.

This requirement for consent in governance shows itself most plainly in civic societies through the voting franchise, because the "power of elections has ever been regarded as a point of the last consequence to all free governments." Some citizens "who live dependent upon the will of others" cannot participate in elections, including "those who are under age, and therefore incapable of judging; those who are convicted of perjury or subornation of perjury, and therefore unworthy of judging; and those who obtain their freeholds by fraudulent conveyances, and would therefore vote to serve infamous purposes."

Those excluded from the "great privilege" of voting are naturally "subject to the undue influence of their superiors." In the case of children and the incarcerated, we accept this as a given. But why, Wilson ponders, are all American colonists also placed into such categories? After a quick history lesson on the rights of British citizens in America, he reminds the reader that consent to laws comes through legislative representatives, and that

---

6 James Wilson, "Considerations on the Nature and Extent of the Legislative Authority of the British Parliament," in *Collected Works of James Wilson* (1774; Indianapolis: Liberty Fund, 2007), 1:21-38.

> the *sole* reason why [citizens] are bound [to obey acts of the British parliament] is, because the representatives of the commons of Great Britain have given their suffrages in favour of those acts. But are the representatives of the commons of Great Britain the representatives of the Americans? Are they elected by the Americans? Are they such as the Americans, if they had the power of election, would probably elect? Do they know the interest of the Americans?

Despite Wilson's expansion of the taxation complaint against Parliament, he had not yet given up on the established relationship between Britain and its colonies. He continued to accept America's dependence on the Crown, and that as British citizens, there was an expectation of "obedience and loyalty, which the colonists owe to the kings of Great Britain." But the Parliament deserved no such obedience, since the lack of colonial representation in that body meant that "the commons of Great Britain have no dominion over their equals and fellow subjects in America."

JOHN ADAMS
DELEGATE FROM MASSACHUSETTS

John Adams was hesitant to recommend himself as a quality author. He identified Thomas Jefferson as someone who wrote "ten times better than I can," and understood that he (Adams) was "obnoxious, suspected and unpopular" in the eyes of the public.[7] Despite this self-loathing of his own content, Adams was a voracious reader—likely more well-read than Jefferson—and turned out reliable, informed, and well-reasoned revolutionary content at a steady pace.

---

7 From John Adams to Timothy Pickering, Montezillo, August 6, 1822, in *Founders Online: The Adams Papers*, National Archives, https://founders.archives.gov/documents/Adams/99-02-02-7674.

His most influential work, *Thoughts on Government*, appeared in print in April 1776, just months before the break with Great Britain.[8] Published anonymously at the behest of fellow delegate Richard Henry Lee, the text carried on the Platonic tradition of describing the ideal form of government. While not directly relevant to the break with England, the work's content provided some support for the future US Constitution.

The end of good government, Adams begins, is to enable "happiness to the greatest number of persons, and in the greatest degree," and that one form of government, the republic, is the one most likely to bring that outcome to fruition. Republics work because they represent "an empire of laws, and not of men," and use reason and stable governance as substitutes for the more common structure based on fear, which is "so sordid and brutal a passion, and renders men in whose breasts it predominates so stupid and miserable." The text goes on to lift up the virtues of republicanism, especially the benefits of the representative assembly, and the separation of the executive, legislative, and judicial powers. Adams also advocated for the annual selection of legislators, since in his view, "where annual elections end, there slavery begins."

As was the case with other colonial writers, Adams gladly invoked the Enlightenment authors who came before, lifting up by name such luminaries as "Sidney, Harrington, Locke, Milton, Nedham, Neville, Burnet, and Hoadly." He sneered at those Englishmen who rejected the wisdom of these foundational writers, but encouraged those Americans who would seek after a grand republic. It was his firm belief that "a constitution founded on these principles introduces knowledge among the people, and inspires them with a conscious dignity becoming freemen," leading to "good humor, sociability, good manners, and good morals" in the

---

8   John Adams, *Thoughts on Government* (Philadelphia: John Dunlap, 1776).

population, and making "the common people brave and enterprising." Whether America's experiment with republican government led to good manners and morals may be debated among thoughtful people. But Adams's concluding prognostication turned out to be correct: "These colonies, under such forms of government, and in such a union, would be unconquerable by all the monarchies of Europe."

FRANCIS HOPKINSON
DELEGATE FROM NEW JERSEY

The disagreements between Great Britain and the colonies were clearly serious, to the point of violent war and bloodshed. But not every refutation took that stringent tone. Consider the writings of Francis Hopkinson from New Jersey. Although he was willing to risk bankruptcy, imprisonment, and death for his association with the *Declaration*, he was not below using humor to mock his British counterparts.

In his satirical *Translation of a Letter, written by a Foreigner on his Travels*,[9] Hopkinson describes the British as a people who reject any idea of American ascendancy because "he goes into his best parlor, and looks on a map of England, four feet square; on the other side of the room he sees a map of North and South America, not more than two feet square, and exclaims: 'How can these things be! It is altogether impossible!'"

The essay also ridicules the low civic education of those in Great Britain: "Talk to him of the British constitution, he will tell you it is a glorious constitution; ask him what it is, and he is ignorant of its

---

9   Francis Hopkinson, "Translation of a Letter, written by a Foreigner on his Travels," in *A Library of American Literature: Literature of the Revolutionary Period*, ed. Edmund Clarence Stedman and Ellen Mackay Hutchinson (New York: Charles L. Webster & Co., 1888), 3:236-240.

first principles; but he is sure that he can make and sell pin-heads under it.... He believes in the Athanasian Creed, honors the king, and makes pin-heads—and what more can be expected of man?"

He contrasts the poor state of those in Great Britain with the typical American.

> The lowest tradesman [in America] is not without some degree of general knowledge.... They have libraries. Not a tradesman but will find time to read.... He reads political disquisitions and learns the great outlines of his rights as a man and as a citizen.... In a word, he is sure that, notwithstanding the determination of the king, lords, and commons to the contrary, two and two can never make five.

CHAPTER SIX

Distribution

While the *Declaration of Independence* represented the official position of the collective colonies, the nature of its presentation and dissemination was an important part of putting it into effect. Not every missive issued by the Congress was meant for the general public. That body had, for instance, a Committee of Secret Correspondence, charged with advancing the American cause before influential politicians, statesmen, and royalty in Britain, France, Spain, and other locales that could make a difference for the colonies in their fight against Parliament and the king. The Congress had also issued earlier pleas designed for direct presentation to the court of King George, brought there by agents of the colonies, or passed along by the various royal governors.

The *Petition to the King*, published by the earlier 1774 Congress, was such a document, a "loyal address to his Majesty…dutifully requesting the royal attention to the grievances that alarm and distress his Majesty's faithful subjects in North-America, and entreating his Majesty's gracious interposition for the removal of such grievances."[1] Congress approved the completed petition on October 25 of that year, when "two copies of the Address to the King being engrossed and compared were signed at the table by

---

1   *Journals of the Continental Congress, 1774-1789*, ed. Worthington C. Ford et. al. (Washington, DC: Government Printing Office, 1904-37), October 1, 1774, 1:53.

all members." Benjamin Franklin forwarded the document to his agent in London a week later.[2]

The *Declaration* was not such a back-channel dialog. Instead, the delegates opted to "solemnly publish and declare" its contents, not specifically to the king and Parliament, but generally to the American populace. Johannes Gutenberg's printing press had already proven itself a powerful tool for influencing the masses, and ultimately for altering the nature of power, hierarchies, and history. Martin Luther's ideas on the working of grace in believers and the futility of papal indulgences might have remained nothing more than controversial points of debate inside the cloister had not movable type enabled the speedy dissemination of his writings and thoughts. The firewood of printing allowed the flames of the Protestant Reformation to burn through Europe, a marvel given that literacy rates in Germany maxed out at a third of the population.[3]

By the mid-eighteenth century, literacy rates in the colonies were closer to eighty-five percent for males, with variations by wealth, region, and occupation.[4] Books, especially those imported from Europe, were still the domain of the rich. But everyone could access broadsides and newspapers, an easy task when "forty newspapers provided Americans with news, and every colony

---

2   *Journals of the Continental Congress, 1774-1789*, October 26, 1774, 1:113. For an overview of the development and submission of this document, see Edwin Wolf, "The Authorship of the 1774 Address to the King Restudied," *The William and Mary Quarterly* 22, no. 2 (April 1965): 189-224.

3   In Germany, "literacy rates ran between one person in ten and one person in three in the cities, but only at one person in 20 for the population as a whole." See Jean-François Gilmont, ed., *The Reformation and the Book*, trans. Karin Maag (New York: Routledge, 2016), especially the first chapter.

4   The Baptists and other Protestants in New England, with their emphasis on understanding scripture, helped drive colonial literacy even in Anglican regions. See Kenneth A. Lockridge, *Literacy in Colonial New England: An Enquiry into the Social Context of Literacy in the Early Modern West* (New York: W. W. Norton, 1974).

except Vermont had at least one newspaper" by the time of the revolution.[5] When Thomas Paine published *Common Sense* in January 1776, its ideas spread quickly, driven by the power of the argument and by the easy readability of ink on paper. Paine himself estimated that 120,000 copies of the work sold within its first three months on the market.

Formal presentation of the *Declaration* to Parliament and the king would come soon enough, but independence was for the people. Moments after approving the text of the *Declaration*, the Congress ordered that "copies of the declaration be sent to the several assemblies, conventions and committees, or councils of safety, and to the several commanding officers of the continental troops; that it be proclaimed in each of the United States, and at the head of the army."[6] Two days later, the full text of the document appeared on the front page of the *Pennsylvania Evening Post*. In the days following America's official separation from Britain, thirty newspapers across the colonies published the content, sometimes at the cost of their fortunes and safety.[7]

The *Declaration of Independence* was obviously not the endpoint of the American experience, but neither was it the beginning. The reasons for colonial separation from Great Britain did not spring into Jefferson's mind as inspired scripture. Instead, he relied on ideas of natural rights that came into being when the Creator breathed life into man. The members of the Second Continental Congress recognized the truths, as did the Enlightenment writers before them,

---

5 David A. Copeland, *Debating the Issues in Colonial Newspapers* (New York: Greenwood Press, 2000), viii.
6 *Journals of the Continental Congress, 1774-1789*, July 4, 1776, 5:516.
7 For an overview of the newspapers that printed the Declaration, see *Journeys & Crossings*, episode "Publishing the Declaration of Independence," presented by Robin Shields, Library of Congress, published on January 19, 2016, https://www.loc.gov/rr/program/journey/declaration.html.

and the classical authors even further back in time. The founders published the *Declaration of Independence* not simply to announce the patriot decision to break with the British Empire, but to communicate to all Americans the providential rights of life, liberty, and the pursuit of happiness.

APPENDIX A

Signatories by State

The copy of the *Declaration of Independence* approved by the Continental Congress on July 4, 1776, likely had only two signatures, or perhaps none at all.[1] The notes in the convention's official journals are sparse concerning the events of that day, with no specific notation of a signing ceremony. That very evening, Congress passed the initial edition of the document on to John Dunlap, the official printer for Congress. Dunlap published around 200 copies immediately, terminating each with a signature-like notation:

Signed by Order and in Behalf of the Congress,

John Hancock, President.

Attest.

Charles Thompson, Secretary.

Whether the signatures of President Hancock and Secretary Thompson appeared on the paper handed to Dunlap, or simply came to the printer via a verbal command is unknown, since that priceless original copy has been lost to history. What is known is

---

1   Jefferson himself claimed that all delegates, or at least those with the authority and inclination to sign, did so on July 4. In a letter to Samuel W. Wells on May 12, 1819, Jefferson wrote that the *Declaration* "was signed by every member present, except Mr. [John] Dickinson [of Pennsylvania]" on July 4. For an extended discussion of this comment by Jefferson, and how it is likely incorrect, see John H. Hazelton, *The Declaration of Independence: Its History* (New York: Dodd, Mead and Co., 1906), 195-200.

that the engrossed edition of the *Declaration* we admire today had most of its signature block filled in on August 2, nearly a month after the vote to approve the text. By then, some delegates had been shuffled away, replaced by their legislatures for various reasons, including reasons of war.

The lists of delegates below indicate the age of each member at the time they signed. Some of these ages are approximate, due to calendar changes (the transition from the Julian to the Gregorian calendar), confusion as to the birth dates for some delegates, and a lack of documentation concerning when a few of the final signers affixed their names to the parchment.[2]

CONNECTICUT
FOUR SIGNERS

Although only two delegates from Connecticut were present in Congress for the July resolution, a total of four members eventually signed the document.

Samuel Huntington, Age 45

> Strong critic of the Intolerable Acts, president of the Congress when the Articles of Confederation took effect, making him the first President of the United States, albeit under a former constitution.

Roger Sherman, Age 55

> Second oldest member of Congress, after Benjamin Franklin,

---

2   In addition to other signer-specific notations, much of the biographical information in this appendix comes from the following sources: *Encyclopedia Britannica*, www.britannica.com; The Society of the Descendants of the Signers of the Declaration of Independence, http://www.dsdi1776.com/learn-about-the-signers/; Charles Goodrich, *Lives of the Signers to the Declaration of Independence* (Philadelphia: Thomas Desilver, 1831); and *Biographical Dictionary of the United States Congress*, http://bioguide.congress.gov/.

and the only person to sign four key American documents: the Continental Association, the *Declaration of Independence*, the Articles of Confederation, and the US Constitution.

William Williams, Age 45
>Selected as a replacement delegate for fellow signer Oliver Wolcott, when the latter fell ill. Williams arrived in Philadelphia on July 28, and signed when the document appeared nearly a week later.

Oliver Wolcott, Age 49
>Member of Congress since 1775, but became ill in June 1776, missing both the July vote and the August signing. He resumed his place in Congress in November, adding his signature at that time.

DELAWARE
THREE SIGNERS

The initial vote for independence on July 1 lacked complete support, including a split vote from Delaware, with only two of its delegates present. By the next day, the arrival of the colony's third delegate ensured its assent.[3]

Thomas McKean, Age 42
>Head of Delaware's "County party" faction. He missed the August 2 signing due to his war activities, and might have signed as late as 1781, as his name is absent from many printed editions in the years following independence.

---

[3] Some of the biographical information in this section comes from Daniel H. Marchi, *Past Future Power Belongs to the Reserved Power Clause* (Bloomington, IN: AuthorHouse, 2013), 420.

George Read, Age 42

> Head of the opposing "Court party" faction, Read voted against separation from Britain on July 2, but still signed the document when it was presented to Congress on August 2.

Caesar Rodney, Age 47

> Though in Dover during the July 1 vote, Rodney rode all that day and night for Philadelphia—an eighty-mile trip—and arrived, fatigued and ill, but alert enough to break his colony's voting deadlock.

GEORGIA
THREE SIGNERS

Distant and sparsely populated Georgia didn't participate in the First Continental Congress, and had only been an official royal colony since the early 1750s. Although it was far removed from the blunt British actions taking place in colonies like Massachusetts, it still joined with its fellow provinces in the quest for independence.

Button Gwinnett, Age 41

> Born in Great Britain, then came to Georgia with his wife in 1765. After his stint in Congress, he returned to Georgia in early 1777 as governor, and died in a duel with a leading military commander from that state two months later.

Lyman Hall, Age 52

> A clergyman and physician, initially sent to Congress in 1775 as a delegate from one small section of the colony, though he was later upgraded to a full delegate before the vote on independence.

George Walton, Age 25 to 35

> Bitter enemy of Gwinnett, yet the two voted together to

separate from Great Britain. There is wide disagreement as to Walton's birth year, with estimates ranging from 1741 to 1750.

MARYLAND
FOUR SIGNERS

Maryland, as a colony, leaned loyalist, and the delegates it sent to the second Congress were instructed "that you do not, without the previous knowledge and approbation of the convention of this province, assent to any proposition to declare these colonies independent of the crown of Great Britain... [unless] absolutely necessary for the preservation of the liberties of the united colonies."[4] But as the situation with England progressed over 1776, the colony had a change of heart, and on June 28, it provided new instructions to its delegates, authorizing them to vote for independence.[5]

One delegate, John Rogers, voted for the resolution on July 2. A subsequent illness forced him to return to Annapolis before the August 2 signing, making him the only assenting delegate not to sign the final document.[6]

Charles Carroll of Carrollton, Age 38

The only Roman Catholic to sign the *Declaration*, Carroll was a leading member of Maryland's revolutionary government, selected on July 4 to replace the ailing John Rogers.[7] He

---

4 "In Convention, January 12, 1776," in *Proceedings of the Convention of the Province of Maryland*, vol. 78, *1774-1776* (Baltimore: James Lucas & E. K. Deaver, 1836), 82-84.
5 "Friday, July 4, 1776," *Proceedings of the Conventions of the Province of Maryland*, 78:176.
6 "Hall of Fame Inductees: John Rogers," Prince George's County Historical Society, http://pghistory.org/main/hall-of-fame/.
7 "Thursday, July 4, 1776," *Proceedings of the Conventions of the Province of Maryland*, 78:189.

arrived in Philadelphia on July 18, before the August signing, and was the last surviving signer after John Adams and Thomas Jefferson passed away.

Samuel Chase, Age 35

After his stint in Congress, Chase went on to become an associate justice of the United States Supreme Court. He was the only member of that court throughout America's history to have been impeached by the House of Representatives, though he was not removed.[8]

William Paca, Age 35

Lawyer and judge from Maryland, rising to chief justice before becoming governor of that state. Paca also started the local Sons of Liberty branch in Annapolis.

Thomas Stone, Age 32 or 33

Although Maryland had restricted its members from voting for independence from Great Britain, Stone voted for John Adams's independence-minded preamble on May 15, declaring the Crown's authority over each colony to be at an end.[9]

MASSACHUSETTS
FIVE SIGNERS

Massachusetts was, by many measures, the epicenter of anti-America activities by British officials and troops. So it comes as no surprise that many of the most impassioned voices for liberty came to Congress from that colony.

---

8   Will Giles, "The Curious Case of Samuel Chase," *Duke Political Review*, October 30, 2013, http://dukepoliticalreview.org/the-curious-case-of-samuel-chase/.

9   Conway Whittle Sams and Elihu Samuel Riley, *The Bench and Bar of Maryland: A History, 1634 to 1901* (Chicago: Lewis Publishing Co., 1901), 1:174.

John Adams, Age 40

> Lawyer, statesman, future president, and one of the most vocal advocates for American independence, Adams wrote the original preamble for Richard Henry Lee's resolution on independence, which led to the *Declaration*. Adams also published several important works related to the struggle with Britain, and developed the Model Treaty, the document used by Congress to establish relations with other nations.[10]

Samuel Adams, Age 53

> John's cousin Samuel, though not as widely read as John, had the rambunctious Adams reputation for confronting the abuses of the Crown and Parliament. He likely wrote the bulk of the *Massachusetts Circular Letter* in 1768, the document that helped touch off Britain's main frustration with Boston and its citizens. He also had a hand in the *Boston Pamphlet* of 1772, another key revolutionary document.[11]

Elbridge Gerry, Age 32

> Though perhaps best remembered today as the source of the term "gerrymandering," Gerry proved instrumental in developing the Bill of Rights attached to the current US Constitution. He missed the signing on August 2, and had to affix his name later.

John Hancock, Age 40

> Hancock, a protégé of Sam Adams,[12] acted as president of

---

10 "The Model Treaty, 1776," US State Department, Office of the Historian, https://history.state.gov/milestones/1776-1783/model-treaty.
11 "The Formation of the Committees of Correspondence," Massachusetts Historical Society, https://www.masshist.org/revolution/committees.php.
12 "A Politician in Massachusetts," Samuel Adams Heritage Society, http://www.samuel-adams-heritage.com/biography/politician-in-massachusetts.html.

the Congress at the time it published the *Declaration*. A merchant and importer by trade, he held one of the largest fortunes in America during the 1770s.

Robert Treat Paine, Age 45

Paine traced his family's American experience back to the Mayflower. A lawyer and part-time preacher, his participation in the First Continental Congress included the development and transmittal of the *Olive Branch Petition* to King George, an earlier attempt at reconciliation.

NEW HAMPSHIRE
THREE SIGNERS

Originally an extension of the Massachusetts Bay Colony, New Hampshire was used to having its identity modified by Britain from afar. King Charles II separated the two jurisdictions in 1679 by charter, though it lapsed. A new charter under William and Mary in 1691 divided them once more, though they continued to share governors until George II made the divide permanent in 1741.[13]

Josiah Bartlett, Age 46

After first dissolving the provincial legislature in June 1774 for behavior "inconsistent with his Majesty's service," Governor John Wentworth singled out Josiah Bartlett for censure, revoking the judicial and military commissions that Wentworth himself had granted in the 1760s.[14]

---

13 Introduction to *Laws of New Hampshire*, vol. 2, *Province Period: 1702-1745*, ed. Albert Stillman Batchellor (Concord, NH: Rumford Printing Co., 1913), xi-l.

14 For the quote from Wentworth, see *New Hampshire Provincial Papers*, vol. 7, *1761 to 1776* (Nashua, NH: Orren C. Moore, State Printer, 1878), 366-367. For the impact on Bartlett, see *History of Essex County, Massachusetts*, ed. Duane Hamilton Hurd (Philadelphia: J. W. Lewis & Co., 1887), 2:1857.

Matthew Thornton, Age 62

> Irish-born Thornton, a doctor (as was Bartlett), was not elected to the Congress until September 1776, and signed the document when he arrived in Philadelphia in November, three months after most other delegates.

William Whipple, Age 46

> Whipple, a merchant before the war, went on to lead the troops into battle, rising to Brigadier General. As a skilled mathematician and member of the American Philosophical Society, he participated in measuring the 1769 transit of Venus, an experiment that enabled scientists to more accurately determine the distance between the earth and the sun.[15]

NEW JERSEY
FIVE SIGNERS

The congressional delegation representing New Jersey in early 1776 opposed separation from Britain. As the months progressed, the colony was having a change of heart, leaning ever closer to independence. On June 21, as the *Declaration* was under development, New Jersey replaced its entire slate of delegates with a group that would vote in line with the other colonies.[16]

Abraham Clark, Age 50

> During the war, British soldiers captured one or more of Clark's sons, and promised their release if Clark recanted his signature on the *Declaration*; he refused. The story may be

---

15 John Sanderson, *Sanderson's Biography of the Signers to the Declaration of Independence*, rev. ed. Robert T. Conrad (Philadelphia: Thomas, Cowperthwait & Co., 1847), 203.
16 Daniel H. Marchi, *Past Future Power Belongs to the Reserved Power Clause*, 354.

apocryphal, but it represents some of the real dangers experienced by the signers.[17]

John Hart, Age 62 to 70

John Hart was a long-time member of the New Jersey assembly, but he participated in the Continental Congress for just two months, long enough to vote and sign, before leaving on August 30. Experts differ widely on the date and circumstances of his birth.

Francis Hopkinson, Age 38

Originally employed by the Crown as a customs commissioner, Hopkinson later served on the Navy Board in Philadelphia. He may also have been the primary designer of the Great Seal of the United States.[18]

Richard Stockton, Age 45

Captured by loyalists on November 30, 1776, and turned over to the British for five weeks until George Washington was able to negotiate his release. Stockton suffered ill health for two years due to his treatment, and died of cancer in 1781, after most of his worldly possessions had been burned, stolen, or destroyed by the British.

John Witherspoon, Age 53

Scottish-born John Witherspoon moved to America in 1768 to become president of the College of New Jersey, now Princeton. He opposed the Crown's insertion into Ameri-

---

17 Denise Kiernan and Joseph D'Agnese, "Road to Revolution," *New Jersey Monthly*, June 15, 2010, https://njmonthly.com/articles/jersey-living/road-to-revolution/.
18 *Journals of the Continental Congress, 1774-1789*, ed. Worthington C. Ford et. al. (Washington, DC: Government Printing Office, 1904-37), October 27, 1780, 18:984.

can politics and (as a Presbyterian clergyman) the increasing power of the episcopate over protestant institutions. Appointed as chaplain of the Congress by John Hancock, he was the only active clergyman to sign.[19]

NEW YORK
FOUR SIGNERS

New York was the laggard colony, abstaining from the July 2 vote for independence, and the July 4 approval of the *Declaration* that followed. The colony officially provided its support on July 9, after receiving updated instructions from the New York legislature.

Several other delegates from New York were present at the July 2 vote, but absent when it came time to sign in August, having been recalled back the colony: John Alsop, George Clinton, Henry Wisner, and also Robert R. Livingston, a member of the Committee of Five.[20]

William Floyd, Age 41

> A member of the First Continental Congress and the youngest member of the New York delegation to sign the *Declaration*. British troops took control of his estate for the entirety of the war, forcing his family to escape to Connecticut.

Francis Lewis, Age 63

> A Wales-born immigrant to New York, Lewis had been taken prisoner and sent to France during the French and Indian

---

19 Gideon Mailer, *John Witherspoon's American Revolution* (Chapel Hill, NC: University of North Carolina Press, 2017). See especially Mailer's discussion of Witherspoon's 1776 sermon, "The Dominion of Providence Over the Passions of Men."

20 Emily Sneff, "Unsullied by Falsehood: No John Trumbull," Harvard University, *Course of Human Events* (blog), June 27, 2016, https://declaration.fas.harvard.edu/blog/trumbull. This source also includes the mention of when New York delegate Lewis Morris signed the document.

War. The British arrested his wife during the Revolutionary War, and her death stemmed from mistreatment during her confinement.

Philip Livingston, Age 60

A member of the New York assembly going back to 1759, later serving as president of the unofficial New York Provincial Congress when it was formed in 1775.

Lewis Morris, Age 50

Morris's father had served as the first governor of New Jersey after that colony's full separation from New York in 1738.[21] But Morris the son was New York-born, and served in that colony's assembly from 1769. He signed the *Declaration* on or before September 8.

NORTH CAROLINA
THREE SIGNERS

Although North Carolina had an official legislature, conflicts with Governor Josiah Martin led many of its members to form a separate, extra-legal assembly, the North Carolina Provincial Congress, starting in August 1774. The infuriated Martin ultimately dissolved the legal assembly in April 1775, and it was the other, unofficial body that provided delegates to the national Congress.[22]

Joseph Hewes, Age 46

As a member of the earlier First Continental Congress, Hewes had helped craft a list of colonial rights that provided

---

21 Edwin P. Tanner, *The Province of New Jersey, 1664-1738* (New York: Columbia University, 1908), 240ff.
22 Samuel A. Ashe, *History of North Carolina: 1584 to 1783* (Greensboro, NC, 1908).

some of the underlying justifications for the *Declaration* drafted during the subsequent Congress.

William Hooper, Age 34

Originally a loyalist, Hooper supported the royal government in North Carolina, and even fought on the side of Governor William Tyron against some local rebels during the 1771 Battle of Alamance. By 1773, he had taken up the patriot cause.[23]

John Penn, Age 35

Once a lawyer from Virginia, Penn found himself on the wrong side of royal law when he was charged with disrespecting the king after making casual comments about taxation. He was fined a penny by a sympathetic judge, but still refused to pay.

PENNSYLVANIA
NINE SIGNERS

Pennsylvania's internal politics helped make the American resolve for independence a nail-biter up until the July 2 vote. Proprietary Governor John Penn (not the one from North Carolina) and the legislative leaders in that colony were less stressed by Britain's advances, partly from a desire maintain the Penn family charter rights. But when Congress resolved that "the exercise of every kind of authority under the said crown should be totally suppressed,"[24] Pennsylvania's more radical leaders, some of whom were delegates

---

23 Arthur Steinberg, "William Hooper (1742-1790)," John Locke Foundation, *North Carolina History Project*, http://northcarolinahistory.org/encyclopedia/william-hooper-1742-1790/.

24 From John Adams's preamble to Lee's resolution on independence. See *Journals of the Continental Congress, 1774-1789*, May 15, 1776, 4:358.

to the national Congress, saw an opportunity to move the colony closer to independence.

When the first vote for separation from Britain took place on July 1, the divided Pennsylvania delegation voted as a block against the resolution. But when a second vote took place the next day, John Dickinson and Robert Morris, who had opposed the measure the first time, absented themselves from the chamber so that the balance of the colony's vote switched to the affirmative. Morris eventually added his name to the *Declaration*.[25]

Along with Dickinson, two other delegates present during the July 2 vote, Charles Humphreys and Thomas Willing, did not sign the final document. Opposed to the resolution for independence, they left the Congress or were not included in the updated delegation present during the August signing.[26]

George Clymer, Age 37

> An early leader in opposition to British tax laws such as the Stamp Act, and one of the first delegates to call for independence from Britain. Clymer served as one of the Congress's treasurers.

Benjamin Franklin, Age 71

> The "First American" and perhaps the most well-known of all colonists, even among those in the British Isles. He served on the Committee of Five that drafted the *Declaration*, though his input was limited to some editorial changes.

Robert Morris, Age 42

> Though he opposed the July vote for independence, England-born Morris was nonetheless a strong supporter of

---

25 David Lefer, *The Founding Conservatives* (New York: Sentinel, 2013), 118.
26 A. A. Humphreys, "Charles Humphreys," *The Pennsylvania Magazine of History and Biography* 1, no. 1 (1877): 83-85.

the colonial cause. Known as the "Financier of the Revolution," he put his own fortune and his company's ships at the nation's disposal during the war.

John Morton, Age 50 or 51

Morton provided an essential swing vote for Pennsylvania, as he had opposed separation from Great Britain right up until the July 1 vote. He died of an illness less than a year after that vote, the first signer to pass away.

George Ross, Age 46

A lawyer by profession and the uncle of Betsy Ross (of flag-making lore),[27] Ross served as vice president of the First Continental Congress.

Benjamin Rush, Age 30

A noted American doctor and scientist, Rush served as Surgeon General of the Continental Army during the Revolutionary War.

James Smith, Age 56

Another foreign-born delegate, Smith emigrated with his family from Ireland in 1727, when he was still a youth. He participated in Pennsylvania's own constitutional convention, in 1776.

George Taylor, Age 50 or 60

Taylor was born in Ireland, like James Smith, but came over as an indentured servant to a Pennsylvania ironmaster, when he was 20 years old.

---

27 Gene Langley, "The Legend and Truth of Betsy Ross," *The Christian Science Monitor*, June 14, 2002.

James Wilson, Age 33

    Wilson's birth in Scotland puts a full one-third of the Pennsylvania signing delegation within the foreign-born camp. He had only been in America for a decade before signing the *Declaration*.

RHODE ISLAND
TWO SIGNERS

Rhode Island's royal charter granted that colony a level of freedom in governance not available in the other British colonies in America. It retained the right to appoint its own governor, dictate its international trade situation, and pass fairly powerful internal laws as long as they were not "contrary or repugnant" to the laws of England.[28]

But it wasn't a bulletproof document, as proven by the temporary suspension of the charter by James II in the late 1680s. Despite the level of management it had over its own destiny, the impact of Britain's increased presence in the Americas hit Rhode Island just as it did the other future states. This is part of the reason why, in June 1772, citizens of that colony attacked the royal customs ship *Gaspee*, the first significant physical conflict between America and Britain.[29]

William Ellery, Age 48

    A late arrival to the Congress, Ellery took his seat in mid-May, just before the July vote. He replaced delegate Samuel

---

28 "The Charter Granted by King Charles II," *The Public Laws of the State of Rhode-Island and Providence Plantations* (Providence, RI: Miller & Hutchens, 1822), 3-16.

29 Patrick T. Conley and Robert G. Flanders, Jr., *The Rhode Island State Constitution* (New York: Oxford University Press, 2011), 8-9, 15.

Ward, who had died of smallpox while still serving in the Congress.

Stephen Hopkins, Age 69

Hopkins authored *The Rights of Colonies Examined*, an important 1764 pamphlet responding to the Stamp Act. He left Congress soon after signing the *Declaration*, due to poor health.

SOUTH CAROLINA
FOUR SIGNERS

When the first vote for independence took place on July 1, South Carolina voted against the resolution. With Pennsylvania also voting no, New York abstaining, and Delaware deadlocked, that initial vote was far from unanimous. By the next day, South Carolina had a change of heart, perhaps due to editorial promises over the anti-slavery sections of Jefferson's draft *Declaration*.[30]

Thomas Heyward, Jr., Age 30

A lawyer who took his training in England, Heyward served as a local judge during the war. In 1780, British troops took him prisoner during a battle in Charleston, and held him in Florida for nearly a year.

Thomas Lynch, Jr., Age 26

Lynch was elected to the Congress in March 1776, replacing his father who had suffered a sudden stroke.[31] The son was also ill from fever, and the pair headed home just months after the signing. Lynch's father died on the way, and Lynch

---

30 John Ferling, *Independence: The Struggle to Set America Free* (New York: Bloomsbury Press, 2011), 333.
31 *Journal of the Provincial Congress of South Carolina, 1776* (Charlestown, SC: South Carolina Congress, 1776), 101.

himself died two years later at sea, while traveling to Europe to convalesce.

Arthur Middleton, Age 34

Like Thomas Heyward, Middleton trained as a lawyer in England, and like Heyward and Rutledge, he was captured by the British in Charleston and held for nearly a year.

Edward Rutledge, Age 26

Yet another London-trained lawyer from South Carolina, Rutledge was the youngest member of Congress to sign the *Declaration*. His brother John had been a delegate earlier, but was replaced by Thomas Heyward, Jr.

VIRGINIA
SEVEN SIGNERS

The oldest and largest of the British colonies in America, Virginia began its existence with the permanent settlement at Jamestown, in 1607. Its importance was due not just to its population—at nearly a half-million citizens, it was almost twice as large as Pennsylvania, the next largest—but also to its financial power, thanks to its tobacco and its network of British-style gentry.[32] The colony's importance was so universally recognized that, when it came time to draft the *Declaration*, John Adams insisted, "you are a Virginian, and a Virginian ought to appear at the head of this business," as one of the key reasons why Thomas Jefferson should write the document.[33]

---

32 "Population in the Colonial and Continental Periods," chap. 1, in *A Century of Population Growth: From the First Census of the United States to the Twelfth, 1790-1900* (Washington, DC: US Bureau of the Census, 1909), 9, table 1.

33 From John Adams to Timothy Pickering, Montezillo, August 6, 1822, in *Founders Online: The Adams Papers*, National Archives, https://founders.archives.gov/documents/Adams/99-02-02-7674.

Carter Braxton, Age 39

> Although not a loyalist, Braxton was sympathetic to the British position, and considered America's quest for independence to be premature. His place in Congress came suddenly, when he was chosen to replace Peyton Randolph, who died during his tenure. Braxton left the congressional delegation soon after signing the *Declaration* in August 1776.

Benjamin Harrison, Age 50

> The father and great-grandfather of two future presidents, Harrison served as the chairman of the Board of War during his time in the Continental Congress.

Thomas Jefferson, Age 33

> Jefferson always viewed his work on the *Declaration* as a key event in his life. At his request, the inscription on his tombstone lists the document as one of his three great accomplishments, alongside his crafting of the *Virginia Statute for Religious Freedom*, and his role as the father of the University of Virginia.

Francis Lightfoot Lee, Age 41

> Mark Twain described Francis Lightfoot Lee, brother of fellow signer Richard Henry Lee, as a model legislator, who "defiled himself with no juggling, or wire-pulling, or begging" in his public service, but "during four of the darkest years of the Revolution he labored with all his might for his country's best behests."[34]

Richard Henry Lee, Age 44

> Lee famously introduced the resolution for American inde-

---

34 Samuel Clemens, "Francis Lightfoot Lee," in *The Pennsylvania Magazine of History and Biography* 1, no. 3 (1877): 343-5.

pendence to the Congress on June 7, 1776. Although he was not present during the July vote, he returned to Congress the following month, and added his signature to the *Declaration* on September 4.[35]

Thomas Nelson, Jr., Age 37

After attending college in England, Nelson returned to Virginia to work in the family mercantile business. Though an illness removed him from Congress in the spring of 1776, he returned to sign the *Declaration* after its presentation in August.[36]

George Wythe, Age 49 to 50

A lawyer and professor, Wythe trained a young Thomas Jefferson in the practice of the law. He took his place in the Congress in September 1775, adding his signature to the document one year later, after most others had signed.

OTHERS
TWO OFFICIALS

Two other participants in the Second Continental Congress played key roles in bringing forth the *Declaration*. Though they were both citizens of Pennsylvania and prominent leaders in the move toward independence, they were not selected as delegates to the Congress.

Charles Thomson, Age 46

Thomson served as the official congressional Secretary at the time of the vote on independence, and helped establish

---

[35] "Lee Brother Signers," *Stratford Hall*, The Robert E. Lee Memorial Association, http://www.stratfordhall.org/meet-the-lee-family/lee-brother-signers/.

[36] John Sanderson, *Sanderson's Biography of the Signers to the Declaration of Independence*, 630.

relations with foreign powers on behalf of the Congress.[37] In his role as secretary, his name appeared alongside John Hancock's name on the first published broadsides of the *Declaration*.

Timothy Matlack, Age 40

An assistant to Charles Thomson, Matlack's skilled penmanship earned him the privilege of producing the engrossed copy on which the delegates affixed their signatures.[38]

---

37 Lewis R. Harley, *Life of Charles Thomson* (Philadelphia: George W. Jacobs & Co., 1900), 105.
38 Gaillard Hunt, "The Penmanship of the Declaration of Independence," *The Youth's Companion*, June 29, 1916.

APPENDIX B

Enlightenment Sources

Thomas Jefferson's views on natural rights and liberty came about in part through his extensive reading of classical and Enlightenment texts. His passion for acquiring books might be called obsessive today. After the British burned the down the Library of Congress during the War of 1812, the nearly 7,000 books in Jefferson's personal collection became the foundation of the rebuilt reference organization.[1]

Not every item in his library provided a scholarly analysis of unalienable rights or of the law of nations. Jefferson also enjoyed the whimsical series of novels *Tristram Shandy*, and he and his wife Martha would copy out memorable lines from the stories.[2] But the books that guided his thoughts on freedom and government were certainly included. The items below would have been familiar to Jefferson and his compatriots, and together they provide an introduction to the philosophies and ideas that were bringing those in Congress and the entire nation to the perspective expressed in the *Declaration*.

---

1 "Jefferson's Library," Library of Congress, Thomas Jefferson Exhibit, https://www.loc.gov/exhibits/jefferson/jefflib.html.
2 "Lines Copied from Tristram Shandy by Martha and Thomas Jefferson, [before 6 September 1782]," The *Papers of Thomas Jefferson*, vol. 6, *21 May 1781 to 1 March 1784*, ed. Julian P. Boyd (Princeton: Princeton University Press, 1952), 196–197.

The Bible

The Christian scriptures predate the Enlightenment by millennia, but they proved to be an essential foundation for the colonial view of natural law. As the Creator and the Supreme Lawgiver, the biblical God embodies the providential source of natural rights, and therefore, provides eternal authority for America's just stance against the oppressive forces of Great Britain. The ranks of patriots in young America included seminary professors, moderate Christians, and the likes of Thomas Paine, whose anti-Christian book *Age of Reason* nearly cost him all the goodwill he gained from *Common Sense*. But even among those, like Jefferson, who doubted the Gospel message, biblical modes of thought provided the common language through which they validated many Enlightenment beliefs.

The Republic, by Plato (c. 380 BC)

Plato was a fifth-to-fourth century BC thinker who provided the foundation on which virtually all Western philosophical writings rest. Appearing between his mentor Socrates and his student Aristotle, Plato's influence extended thousands of years forward, all the way into the colonial era. His most political work is arguably *The Republic*, written around 380 BC. The book is an attempt to define the nature of true justice, and through the mouthpiece of Socrates, Plato lifts up a meticulously crafted society led by a philosopher-king.

By modern standards, his proposed government has a totalitarian feel. But the effort is an important demonstration that a solid government structure, even if it isn't the one proposed by Plato, can be examined and understood through reason. Three other works by Plato—*Gorgias*, *Minos*, and the

Laws—touch on various aspects of the political realm, including the nature of the law, the source of natural rights, and the overlap between morality, laws, and rights.

Nicomachean Ethics, by Aristotle (c. 350 BC)

In this work on the practical aspects of ethics, Aristotle lifts up happiness as the highest aspiration for mankind. This happiness finds its most appropriate source in the exercise of virtues. Although perfect happiness may be out of the reach of man's nature, Aristotle advocates the pursuit of this happiness through the individual and societal acts of virtue and magnanimity (having a great soul).

Whereas Plato had stressed natural law as an inherent aspect of our reality, his most famous student insisted that this theoretical concept must be made real through practical human actions. Aristotle also produced *Politics*, a work that deals directly with how individuals behave in a community, especially within the "polis," the highest form of community.

On the Commonwealth, by Cicero (c. 51 BC)

Though he lived centuries after Plato and Aristotle, Cicero followed their examples and communicated the ideas of *On the Commonwealth* in the structure of a Socratic dialogue. The late Roman politician Scipio Aemilianus took the place of the wise, questioning Socrates, with a parade of combatants having their ideas picked apart and analyzed through a series of discussions covering six books. A key concept in the text is the role of a constitution in a functioning society. The book also stresses the welfare of the people as a primary reason for governments to exist in the first place.

The Roman Historians (c. 50 BC)

The classical biographies and writings of Plutarch, Livy, and other ancient Roman historians and leaders provided a clear differentiation between the haphazard and potentially ruinous world of pure democracy, and the more stable representative-hosted rule of the people as embodied in a republic. Jefferson lifted up Tacitus as his personal Roman muse, and dreamed of a day when ordinary farmers, after a fulfilling day of agriculture and husbandry, would spend their evenings consuming Tacitus and comparable authors in the original Latin and Greek.

Institutes, by Gaius (130–180)

In this textbook on the legal institutions of the Roman Empire, Gaius identifies two sources for the laws of nations: the laws that are common to all mankind, and the laws that are particular to the specific society. While the common laws apply to every people in all places and times, the second set derives from the people themselves, in response to their specific circumstances and needs. These two aspects of the law closely parallel the Enlightenment-era concepts of natural law and consent of the governed.

Summa Theologica, by Thomas Aquinas (1265–1274)

Written as an introduction for theology students, the thousands of pages of Aquinas's *magnum opus* cover topics in philosophy, theology, society, and politics. The text makes extensive use of contemporary and ancient sources, including those, like Plato and Cicero, who would have been lauded by Jefferson and his associates. Although the author was clearly Catholic, his expansion of Plato's concept of a prime mover into a creative "first cause" would have appealed to deists of the Enlightenment era. Aquinas also touches on the topics of natural law and natural rights, and how these connect to God's eternal law.

Dialogus, by William of Ockham (1332–1347)

The Franciscan friar who give us the concept of *Ockham's razor*—that the simplest option is usually the correct one—was not afraid to ruminate on the complexities of life. William of Ockham's extensive writings cover a wide range of philosophical and theological topics, but he also touched on politics. In his *Dialogus*, a multi-volume discussion between a student and his wise master, he advocates for monarchy as the best form of government, but only one where the king's power is restricted by the natural rights of his subjects. Any power the monarch does wield must be for the common good. He also recommended a separation between church and state, since kings have no authority in heaven, and bishops likewise are not authorized to deal with temporal power.

Of The Laws of Ecclesiastical Polity, by Richard Hooker (1594)

Like Aquinas's *Summa*, Hooker's work is primarily focused on theology, crafted as an Anglican response to Puritan theology then in conflict with the positions of the official church. But the book also covers topics of politics and human society, because even as beings with spiritual goals, humans have a natural inclination to live within societies. With this truth in mind, Hooker discusses the nature of eternal and natural laws, including those that are church-specific, and those that rule the lives of individuals within a commonwealth. His ideas on natural law had a strong impact on John Locke when that latter intellectual crafted his treatises on government.

Institutes of the Lawes of England, by Edward Coke (1628–1644)

As a commentary on the laws of England, the writings of British jurist Coke are certainly less accessible than some of the other books that informed the American colonists. But specific portions of Coke's writings had a significant influence on the patriots, especially given that many in Congress were lawyers. Coke's analysis of the "Doctor Bonham Case" from 1610 helped the American's argue against the writs of assistance that came out of the Stamp Act crisis in 1765, legal documents that allowed British customs agents to waltz into any American establishment, looking for evidence of tax evasion.

Leviathan, by Thomas Hobbes (1651)

This entry is yet another work advocating for the natural rights of individuals as the foundation of a society, that is, a "civil and ecclesiastical common-wealth." Hobbes calls such societies "Leviathan," and in the book he describes how such monstrous creatures come into being through *social contracts*, mutual agreements by the members of a society to form a legitimate government over them, for their collective protection. Hobbes insists that the authority for such government comes from the people, but unlike the accepted view among Jefferson's peers, individual authority within a Hobbesian society ends at some point. The ultimate authority is transferred to the sovereign, and this leader (an individual or a congress) possesses ultimate control over the citizens. Hopefully this is for their good, but if not, they have no recourse, for the sovereign has the power of life and death over those who seek to harm Leviathan. Although ideas like separation of powers and freedom of speech are anathema to such a society, *Leviathan*'s support for original natural rights still stirred the intellectual juices of the colonists.

De jure naturae et gentium, by Samuel von Pufendorf (1672)

Hobbes's strong sovereign was necessary, he believed, because men in a state of nature are at war. To mitigate those tendencies, the state must be the final arbiter of what is right behavior. Samuel von Pufendorf, in his book (translated as "On the Law of Nature and of Nations"), agrees with this strong-authority approach, but offers a less rigid view of how a state and society should work, based on his belief that men in a state of nature are a more peace-loving group than that presented by Hobbes.

Discourses Concerning Government, by Algernon Sidney (1680)

In England, the strong sovereign at the heart of Hobbes's contracted society found its justification in the divine right of kings. Not only did the king have ultimate authority, but God himself declared it to be so. Algernon Sidney disagreed, and laid out a critique of the theory in *Discourses Concerning Government*. In the book, Sidney posits that not only are individuals in a state of nature the origin of government, they continue to have the right to define the structure of government, even when the sovereign holds power in a society. This right to abolish a corrupt government and construct it anew implies that the people, and not the sovereign, are the final authority on, well, everything, an unpopular view among kings. Sidney was martyred for his beliefs.

Plato Redivivus, by Henry Neville (1681)

Although most of his writings are classified as satire, Neville's more serious *Plato Redivivus* addresses the dissemination of power within an expanding society. The book, written as a set of dialogues, proposes the division of monarchical power into a set of parliamentary councils, with annually rotating memberships. It was republicanism for monarchies. Naturally, this scenario would not have been the first option for the King of England, but for Americans ready to toss the entire monarchy aside, the book provided a welcome encouragement to implement representative government.

Second Treatise of Government, by John Locke (1689)

It's a bit embarrassing how often John Locke's work comes up when discussing the foundations of the *Declaration*. Yet there is no getting around the fact that his *Second Treatise*, "An Essay Concerning the True Original, Extent and End of Civil Government," eloquently discussed the core elements of a free society: natural law, consent of the governed, representative government, the authority to abolish a corrupt government, and the natural rights of life, liberty, and estate.

"The Nature of the Kingdom of Christ," by Benjamin Hoadly (1717)

Rebuttals to the divine right of kings concept were not limited to political philosophes. Theologians, including English cleric Benjamin Hoadly, provided their own opinions on the practice. In his March 13, 1717, sermon, "The Nature of the Kingdom of Christ," which commenced a national debate known as the Bangorian Controversy, Bishop Hoadly preached that the Bible does not provide support for church government of any sort. It rejected the idea that authority comes from God through specific royal instruments, and eventually down to the people. Instead, God's authority is communicated through the people, and it is from that source that kings come to power.

A Treatise of Human Nature, by David Hume (1739)

> David Hume, a Scottish philosopher and essayist, lived at the same time as many of the signers, and was friends with Benjamin Franklin. His philosophical writings, with their focus on empiricism and human passion, provided a foil to Locke's rationalism. Hume believed that reason was an insufficient tool through which to identify and explain ultimate reality, but that we could instead sense such things intuitively. Some commentators believe that Franklin's *Declaration* edit—from "we hold these truths to be sacred and undeniable" to "we hold these truths to be self-evident"—came about as a result of Hume's influence on Franklin's view of reality.

The Spirit of the Laws, by Montesquieu (1748)

> Building on Locke's foundation, Montesquieu's work discusses the idea of "political liberty," and it recommends the separation of the executive, legislative, and judicial powers into distinct authoritative governmental bodies so as to protect liberty. Montesquieu also discussed more practical concerns, such as freedom of assembly and just penalties for crimes, issues that the patriots would have had in mind in the years before the Revolutionary War.

The Social Contract, by Jean-Jacques Rousseau (1762)

> Like Montesquieu, Rousseau believed that man in a non-governmental state of nature is also in a state of peace, but that once interactions and societies form, the tendency is for war. Therefore governments exist to protect the rights of the people who make up a society. The format of the titular *social contract* shows that the authority to protect such rights comes entirely from the people, and not from the chosen sovereign. Even though the government has the power to coerce,

through its armies and laws, that power is not by right. The only legitimate authority is one that comes from the people, and they obtain it by natural right.

Commentaries on the Laws of England, by William Blackstone (1765)

In this influential treatise on the British constitution and common law, Blackstone deftly joins the philosophical concepts of John Locke with the dictates of the legal system. The first two sections of his work, "The Rights of Persons" and "The Rights of Things," provide a legal analysis of the natural rights of life, liberty, and the pursuit of happiness (including through private property), and explain how societal law exists to support these rights.

The Wealth of Nations, by Adam Smith (1776)

Although the 1776 publication of *An Inquiry into the Nature and Causes of the Wealth of Nations* likely places it too late to have impacted the *Declaration*, the free-market ideas it advocated, especially where they conflicted with Britain's mercantilism, were not unwelcome to the founders.[3] Smith, a Scottish intellectual, wrote during the influential Scottish Enlightenment, and the ideas that came out of that movement floated to America's shores not only from writers like Smith, but also from prominent members of Congress with Scottish roots. This included John Witherspoon, a signer from New Jersey who immigrated to America from that region of the British Empire.

---

[3] Samuel Fleischacker, "Adam Smith's Reception among the American Founders, 1776-1790," *The William and Mary Quarterly* 59, no. 4 (October 2002): 897-924.

APPENDIX C

Bibliography

Acts and Ordinances of the Interregnum, 1642-1660. Edited by C. H. Firth and R. S. Rait. 3 vols. London: His Majesty's Stationery Office, 1911.

The Acts and Resolves, Public and Private, of the Province of the Massachusetts Bay. Edited by A. C. Goodell et. al. 21 vols. Boston: Wright & Potter, Printers, 1869.

"The Act of Abjuration." Translated in *A Fourth Collection of Scarce and Valuable Tracts*. London, 1751.

Adams Family Correspondence. Edited by L. H. Butterfield et. al. 10 vols. Cambridge, MA: Harvard University Press and Boston: Massachusetts Historical Society, 1963-2011.

The Adams Papers. Massachusetts Historical Society: https://www.masshist.org/adams_editorial/.

Adams, James, Samuel Niles, Norton Quincey, James Penniman, and John Hayward. "Instructions Adopted by the Braintree Town Meeting." September 24, 1765. In *Papers of John Adams*. Volume 1. Boston: Massachusetts Historical Society, 1977, 137-140.

Adams, John. *Founders Online: The Adams Papers*. National Archives. https://founders.archives.gov/about/Adams.

Adams, John. *Legal Papers of John Adams*. Edited by L. Kinvin Wroth and Hiller B. Zobel. 3 vols. Boston: Massachusetts Historical Society, 1965.

Adams, John. *Novanglus; or, A History of the Dispute with America, From Its Origin, in 1754, to the Present Time*. In *The Papers of John*

Adams. Volume 2. 1775; Boston: Massachusetts Historical Society, 1977, 216-385.

Adams, John. *Papers of John Adams*. Edited by Robert J. Taylor et. al. 16 vols. Boston: Massachusetts Historical Society, 1977-2012.

Adams, John. *Thoughts on Government*. Philadelphia: John Dunlap, 1776.

Adams, John. "Two Replies of the Massachusetts House of Representatives to Governor Hutchinson." In *The Revolutionary Writings of John Adams*. Edited by C. Bradley Thompson. 1772; Indianapolis: Liberty Fund, 2000.

Adams, John. *Works of John Adams*. Edited by Charles Francis Adams. 10 vols. Boston: Little, Brown and Co., 1856.

American Archives. Edited by M. St. Clair Clark and Peter Force. 9 vols. Washington, DC, 1837, http://amarch.lib.niu.edu/.

Andrews, Charles M. "The Royal Disallowance." In *Proceedings of the American Antiquarian Society* 24 (October 1914): 342-362.

Aquinas, Thomas. *Scriptum super libros Sententiarium* [Commentary on the Sentences of Peter Lombard]. In *Select Political Writings*. Translated by J. G. Dawson. Edited by A. P. d'Entrèves. Oxford: Basil Blackwell, 1948.

Aristotle. *Nicomachean Ethics*.

Aristotle. *Politics*. In *Aristotle in 23 Volumes*. Translated by H. Rackham. Volume 21. Cambridge, MA, Harvard University Press, 1944.

Aristotle. *Rhetoric*. Translated by Michael Pakaluk. Princeton, NJ: The Witherspoon Institute, 2012.

Article signed Candidus. *Boston Gazette*, October 14, 1771. In *The Writings of Samuel Adams*. Volume 2, *1770 to 1773*. Edited by Harry Alonzo Cushing. New York: G. P. Putnam's Sons, 1906.

Ashe, Samuel A. *History of North Carolina: 1584 to 1783*. Greensboro, NC, 1908.

BIBLIOGRAPHY

Bacon, Francis. *Novum Organum.*

Baron de Montesquieu (Charles Louis de Secondat). *The Spirit of the Laws.* Translated in *The Complete Works of M. de Montesquieu.* 4 vols. 1748; London, 1777.

Beer, George Louis, *British Colonial Policy, 1754-1765.* 1907. Reprint, New York: Macmillan Co., 1922.

Berkeley, Lord John, and Sir George Carteret. "The Concession and Agreement of the Lords Proprietors of the Province of New Caesarea, or New Jersey, to and With All and Every the Adventurers and All Such as Shall Settle or Plant There." In *Documents Relating to the Colonial History of the State of New Jersey, 1631-1776.* Edited by William A. Whitehead. 10 vols. Newark, NJ: The Daily Journal, 1880.

Bernard, Francis. *The Papers of Francis Bernard.* Edited by Colin Nicolson. Boston: The Colonial Society of Massachusetts, 2015.

Biographical Dictionary of the United States Congress. http://bioguide.congress.gov/.

Blackstone, William. *Commentaries on the Laws of England.* 4 vols. Oxford, 1765-1769.

Boston Chronicle. September 26, 1768.

Boston Gazette. September 26, 1768, Supplement (Extraordinary).

Braxton, Carter. "An Address to the Convention of the Colony of Ancient Dominion of Virginia." Philadelphia: John Dunlap in Market-Street, 1776.

British History Online. http://www.british-history.ac.uk/.

Carpenter, A. H. "Naturalization in England and the American Colonies." *The American Historical Review* 9, no. 1 (January 1904): 290.

"The Charter Granted by King Charles II." *The Public Laws of the State of Rhode-Island and Providence Plantations.* Providence, RI: Miller & Hutchens, 1822.

"The Charter of the Province of the Massachusetts Bay in New England, 1691." *The Charters and General Laws of the Colony and Province of Massachusetts Bay.* Boston: T. B. Wait, 1814, 18-37.

Chinard, Gilbert. "Thomas Jefferson as a Classical Scholar." *The American Scholar* 1, no. 2 (Spring 1932): 133-143.

Cicero. *On the Commonwealth.*

Cicero. *On the Laws.*

Clemens, Samuel. "Francis Lightfoot Lee." In *The Pennsylvania Magazine of History and Biography* 1, no. 3 (1877): 343-5.

Cobbett's Parliamentary History of England. Edited by W. Cobbett et. al. 36 vols. London: R. Bagshaw, 1806-1820.

Colonial and State Records of North Carolina. Edited by William L. Saunders et. al. 30 vols. Raleigh, NC: P. M. Hale, Printer to the State, 1886-1905.

Colonial Origins of the American Constitution: A Documentary History. Edited by Donald S. Lutz. Indianapolis: Liberty Fund, 1998.

Conley, Patrick T., and Robert G. Flanders, Jr. *The Rhode Island State Constitution.* New York: Oxford University Press, 2011.

Connecticut Digital Archive. http://collections.ctdigitalarchive.org.

Copeland, David A. *Debating the Issues in Colonial Newspapers.* New York: Greenwood Press, 2000.

"Declaration of Rights 1765." In *National Documents: State Papers So Arranged as to Illustrate the Growth of our Country from 1606 to the Present Day.* New York: Unit Book Publishing Co., 1906.

Documents of the City of Boston for the Year 1886. 3 vols. Boston: Rockwell and Churchill, City Printers, 1887.

Documents Relative to the Colonial History of the State of New York. Edited by E. B. O'Callaghan et. al. 26 vols. Albany: Weed, Parsons, and Co., 1856.

"The Dutch Declaration of Independence, 1581." In *The Library of Original Sources*, vol. 5, *9th to 16th Centuries*, 189-197. Edited by Oliver J. Thatcher. Milwaukee: University Research Extension Co., 1907.

Edwards, Jonathan. "The Final Judgment." In *The Works of Jonathan Edwards*. Edited by Anthony Uyl. Volume 2. London: John Childs and Son, 1834.

English Bill of Rights, 1689, 1 W. & M. st. 2, c. 2.

Ferling, John. *Independence: The Struggle to Set America Free*. New York: Bloomsbury Press, 2011.

Fleischacker, Samuel. "Adam Smith's Reception among the American Founders, 1776-1790." *The William and Mary Quarterly* 59, no. 4 (October 2002): 897-924.

"The Formation of the Committees of Correspondence." Massachusetts Historical Society. https://www.masshist.org/revolution/committees.php.

Ganter, Herbert Lawrence. "Jefferson's 'Pursuit of Happiness' and Some Forgotten Men." *The William and Mary Quarterly* 16, no. 4 (October 1936): 558-585.

Giles, Will. "The Curious Case of Samuel Chase." *Duke Political Review*, October 30, 2013. http://dukepoliticalreview.org/the-curious-case-of-samuel-chase/.

Gilmont, Jean-François, ed. *The Reformation and the Book*. Translated by Karin Maag. New York: Routledge, 2016.

Goodrich, Charles A. *Lives of the Signers to the Declaration of Independence*. Philadelphia, 1834.

Graber, Mark A. "State Constitutions and National Constitutions." Legal studies research paper 2016-30, University of Maryland Francis King Carey School of Law, 2016. https://ssrn.com/abstract=2817882.

Graymont, Barbara. *The Iroquois in the American Revolution*. Syracuse, NY: Syracuse University Press, 1972.

Greene, Jack P. *The Quest for Power: The Lower Houses of Assembly in the Southern Royal Colonies, 1689-1776*. Chapel Hill, NC, University of North Carolina Press, 1963.

Griffith, William. *Historical Notes of the American Colonies and Revolution: From 1754 to 1775.* New Jersey, 1843.

Grotius, Hugo. *The Rights of War and Peace.* Book 1, chapter 4, *Of a War made by Subjects against their Superiors,* section 8. Translated by A.C. Campbell. Edited by David J. Hill. 1625; New York: M. Walter Dunne, 1901.

"Hall of Fame Inductees: John Rogers." Prince George's County Historical Society. http://pghistory.org/main/hall-of-fame/.

Hancock, John. "Boston Massacre Oration." A speech delivered in Boston, Massachusetts, March 5, 1774.

Harley, Lewis R. *Life of Charles Thomson.* Philadelphia: George W. Jacobs & Co., 1900.

Hathi Trust Digital Library. https://www.hathitrust.org.

Hazelton, John H. *The Declaration of Independence: Its History.* New York: Dodd, Mead and Co., 1906.

History of Essex County, Massachusetts. Edited by Duane Hamilton Hurd. 2 vols. Philadelphia: J. W. Lewis & Co., 1887.

Hobbes, Thomas. *Leviathan.* London, 1651.

Hopkins, Stephen. *The Rights of Colonies Examined.* Providence, RI, 1764.

Hopkinson, Francis. "Translation of a Letter, written by a Foreigner on his Travels." In *A Library of American Literature: Literature of the Revolutionary Period,* vol. 3, 236-240. Edited by Edmund Clarence Stedman and Ellen Mackay Hutchinson. New York: Charles L. Webster & Co., 1888.

Humphreys, A. A. "Charles Humphreys." *The Pennsylvania Magazine of History and Biography* 1, no. 1 (1877): 83-85.

Hunt, Gaillard. "The Penmanship of the Declaration of Independence." *The Youth's Companion,* June 29, 1916.

Hutchinson, Thomas. *The Correspondence of Thomas Hutchinson.* Edited by John W. Tyler. Boston: The Colonial Society of Massachusetts, 2014.

BIBLIOGRAPHY 179

Hutchinson, Thomas. *Strictures upon the Declaration of the Congress at Philadelphia in a Letter to a Noble Lord.* London, 1776.

Internet Modern History Sourcebook. "American Independence" section. Fordham University. http://sourcebooks.fordham.edu/Halsall/mod/modsbook12.asp.

Isaacson, Walter. *Benjamin Franklin: An American Life.* New York: Simon & Schuster, 2003.

Jefferson, Thomas. *Founders Online: The Papers of Thomas Jefferson.* National Archives. https://founders.archives.gov/about/Jefferson.

Jefferson, Thomas. *The Papers of Thomas Jefferson.* Edited by Julian P. Boyd et. al. 42 vols. Princeton: Princeton University Press, 1950-2016.

Jefferson, Thomas. *A Summary View of the Rights of British America.* Williamsburg, VA, 1774.

Jefferson, Thomas. *The Works of Thomas Jefferson, Federal Edition.* Edited by Paul Leicester Ford. 12 vols. New York and London: G. P. Putnam's Sons, 1904-1905.

Jefferson, Thomas, and John Dickinson, "Declaration of the Causes and Necessity of Taking Up Arms, July 6, 1775." In *Documents Illustrative of the Formation of the Union of the American States.* Edited by Charles C. Tansill. Washington, DC: Government Printing Office, 1927.

"Jefferson's Library." Library of Congress, *Thomas Jefferson Exhibit.* https://www.loc.gov/exhibits/jefferson/jefflib.html.

Jenkinson, Clay. "Presidential Decorum." *The Thomas Jefferson Hour,* June 13, 2017. Podcast, episode 1238. http://jeffersonhour.com/blog/1238.

Journals of the Continental Congress, 1774-1789. Edited by Worthington C. Ford et. al. 34 vols. Washington, DC: Government Printing Office, 1904-1937.

Journals of the House of Burgesses of Virginia. Edited by John Pendleton Kennedy. Richmond, VA, 1905.

Journals of the House of Representatives of Massachusetts. Volume 45, *1768 to 1769.* Boston: Massachusetts Historical Society, 1976.

Journal of the Provincial Congress of South Carolina, 1776. Charlestown, SC: South Carolina Congress, 1776.

Kiernan, Denise, and Joseph D'Agnese. "Road to Revolution." *New Jersey Monthly*, June 15, 2010. https://njmonthly.com/articles/jersey-living/road-to-revolution/.

Kiernan, Denise, and Joseph D'Agnese. *Signing Their Lives Away.* Philadelphia: Quirk Books, 2009.

Kierner, Cynthia A. *Traders and Gentlefolk: The Livingstons of New York, 1675-1790.* Ithaca NY: Cornell University Press, 1992.

King George III. "His Majesty's most gracious speech to both houses of Parliament, on Friday, October 27, 1775." In Library of Congress Printed Ephemera Collection, folio 108, folder 38. https://www.loc.gov/item/rbpe.10803800/.

Langley, Gene. "The Legend and Truth of Betsy Ross." *The Christian Science Monitor*, June 14, 2002.

Laws of New Hampshire. Edited by Albert Stillman Batchellor. 10 vols. Concord, NH: Rumford Printing Co., 1913.

Leamon, James S. *Revolution Downeast: The War for American Independence in Maine.* Amherst, MA: University of Massachusetts Press, 1993.

"Lee Brother Signers." Stratford Hall, The Robert E. Lee Memorial Association. http://www.stratfordhall.org/meet-the-lee-family/lee-brother-signers/.

Lefer, David. *The Founding Conservatives.* New York: Sentinel, 2013.

Leonard, Lewis A. *Life of Charles Carroll of Carrollton.* New York: Moffat, Yard and Co., 1918.

Library of Congress, *Journeys & Crossings.* Episode "Publishing the Declaration of Independence." Published on January 19, 2016. Presented by Robin Shields. https://www.loc.gov/rr/program/journey/declaration.html.

Lilburne, John, William Walwyn, Thomas Prince, and Richard Overton. *An Agreement of the Free People of England.* April 30, 1649.

Lind, John. *Answer to the Declaration of the American Congress.* London, 1776.

Locke, John. *Second Treatise of Government.* Edited by Thomas Hollis. London, 1764.

Lockridge, Kenneth A. *Literacy in Colonial New England: An Enquiry into the Social Context of Literacy in the Early Modern West.* New York: W. W. Norton, 1974.

London Gazette. "By the King, a Proclamation." October 8, 1763.

Lossing, Benson J. *Pictorial Field-Book of the Revolution.* 2 vols. New York: Harper & Brothers, 1850.

Lowell, Edward J. *The Hessians and the Other German Auxiliaries of Great Britain in the Revolutionary War.* New York: Harper & Brothers, 1884.

Lucas, Stephen. "Justifying America: The Declaration of Independence as a Rhetorical Document." In *American Rhetoric: Context and Criticism*, 67-130. Edited by Thomas W. Benson. Carbondale, IL: Southern Illinois University Press, 1989.

Lucas, Stephen. "*The 'Plakkaat van Verlatinge': A Neglected Model for the American Declaration of Independence.*" In *Connecting Cultures: The Netherlands in Five Centuries of Transatlantic Exchange.* Edited by Rosemarijn Hofte and Johanna C. Kardux. Amsterdam: VU University Press, 1994, 189–207.

Maclay, Edgar Stanton. *A History of American Privateers.* New York: D. Appleton and Co., 1899.

Maier, Pauline. *American Scripture: Making the Declaration of Independence.* New York: Knopf, 1997.

Mailer, Gideon. *John Witherspoon's American Revolution.* Chapel Hill, NC: University of North Carolina Press, 2017.

Magna Carta [English]. Davis, G. R. C. *Magna Carta.* London: British Museum, 1963.

Magna Carta [Latin]. *Statutes of the Realm.* Volume 1. London: Dawsons of Pall Mall, 1810-1828, 9-13.

Marchi, Daniel H. *Past Future Power Belongs to the Reserved Power Clause.* Bloomington, IN: AuthorHouse, 2013.

Massachusetts Gazette. "Answer of the Town of Hatfield to the Boston Selectmen." September 23, 1768.

"Mayflower Compact. November 11, 1620." *Documents of American History.* Volume 1. Edited by Henry S. Commager. New York: Appleton-Century Crofts, 1968.

"Message from the House of Representatives, to the Governor, June 30, 1768." In *Speeches of the Governors of Massachusetts from 1765 to 1775 [...].* Boston: Russell and Gardner, 1818.

Miller, John C. *Sam Adams: Pioneer in Propaganda.* 1936; Stanford, CA: Stanford University Press, 1964.

Miller, John C. "The Massachusetts Convention 1768." *New England Quarterly* 7, no. 3 (September 1934): 445-474.

"The Model Treaty, 1776." US State Department, Office of the Historian. https://history.state.gov/milestones/1776-1783/model-treaty.

Montesquieu. *The Spirit of the Laws.* Translated by Thomas Nugent. 1751; New York: Hafner Press, 1949.

Morrison, Jeffrey. "Political Theology in the Declaration of Independence." Lecture presented at James Madison Program in American Ideals and Institutions, Princeton University, April 5-7, 2002.

Mun, Thomas. *England's Treasure by Forraign Trade.* 1664. Reprint, New York: MacMillan Co., 1895.

Natural Law, Natural Rights, and American Constitutionalism. http://www.nlnrac.org.

New Hampshire Provincial Papers. 40 vols. Nashua, NH: Orren C. Moore, State Printer, 1878.

New York Assembly to Henry Moore. Albany, December 15, 1766. Reprinted in "Proceedings of the General Assembly of New York." *The Gentleman's and London Magazine* (May 1767): 267.

New York Journal. "Journal of Occurrences." October 3, 1768.

Online Library of Liberty. http://oll.libertyfund.org.

Otis, James. *The Rights of the British Colonies Asserted and Proved.* Boston & London: J. Almon, 1764.

Papers of King George III. https://www.royalcollection.org.uk/collection/georgian-papers-programme.

Papers of the Continental Congress 1774-1789. National Archives.

The Parliamentary Register. 17 vols. London, 1802.

"A Politician in Massachusetts." Samuel Adams Heritage Society. http://www.samuel-adams-heritage.com/biography/politician-in-massachusetts.html.

"Population in the Colonial and Continental Periods." Chapter 1 in *A Century of Population Growth: From the First Census of the United States to the Twelfth, 1790-1900.* Washington, DC: US Bureau of the Census, 1909.

"Preamble and Resolution of the Virginia Convention, May 15, 1776." In *Documents Illustrative of the Formation of the Union of the American States.* Edited by Charles C. Tansill. Washington, DC: Government Printing Office, 1927.

The Proceedings of the Convention of Delegates, Held at the Capitol, in the City of Williamsburg, in the Colony of Virginia, on Monday the 6th of May, 1776. 1776; Richmond, VA: Ritchie, TrueHeart & Duval, 1816.

Proceedings of the Conventions of the Province of Maryland. Volume 78. Annapolis, MD: James Lucas & E. K. Deaver, 1836.

"A Proclamation by his Excellency the Right Honorable John Earl of Dunmore." *Virginia Gazette (Dixon and Hunter)*, November 25, 1775.

Public Income and Expenditure. Part 2, *Gross Accounts of the United Kingdom, 1801-1869.* London: House of Commons, 1869.

Rhode Island General Assembly. "Act of Renunciation, 1776." In *Virtual Exhibits*, item #68, http://sos.ri.gov/virtualarchives/items/show/68.

"The Rights of the Colonists: A List of Violations of Rights and a Letter of Correspondence." In *The Writings of Samuel Adams*. Volume 2, *1770 to 1773*. Edited by Harry Alonzo Cushing. New York: G. P. Putnam's Sons, 1906.

Riley, Elihu S. *"First Citizen"—Charles Carroll of Carrollton, and "Antilon"—Daniel Dulany, Jr., 1773*. Baltimore: King Bros. State Printers, 1902.

Rowe, Gail Stuart. *Thomas McKean: The Shaping of an American Republicanism*. Boulder, CO: Colorado Associated University Press, 1978.

"Royal Instruction against passing Acts of Naturalization and Divorce." *Documents Relative to the Colonial History of the State of New York*, vol. 8. Edited by E. B. O'Callaghan. Albany, NY: Weed, Parsons and Co., 1857.

Rushworth, John, ed. *Historical Collections of Private Passages of State*. 8 vols. London: D Brown, 1721.

Sams, Conway Whittle, and Riley, Elihu Samuel. *The Bench and Bar of Maryland: A History, 1634 to 1901*. Volume 1. Chicago: Lewis Publishing Co., 1901.

Sanderson, John. *Sanderson's Biography of the Signers to the Declaration of Independence*. Edited by Robert T. Conrad. Revised, Philadelphia: Thomas, Cowperthwait & Co., 1847.

Sharpe, Horatio. *Archives of Maryland: Correspondence of Governor Horatio Sharpe*. Edited by William Hand Brown. 3 (of 14) vols. Baltimore: Maryland Historical Society, 1895.

Sidney, Algernon. *Discourses Concerning Government*. London, 1698.

Smith, Adam. *The Wealth of Nations*. London, 1776.

Sneff, Emily. "Unsullied by Falsehood: No John Trumbull." Harvard University, *Course of Human Events* (blog), June 27, 2016. https://declaration.fas.harvard.edu/blog/trumbull.

The Society of the Descendants of the Signers of the Declaration of Independence. http://www.dsdi1776.com.

Start, Cora. "Naturalization in the English Colonies of America." In *Annual Report of the American Historical Association* (1893): 319-328.

The Statutes at Large of Pennsylvania from 1682 to 1801. 14 vols. Harrisburg, PA, State Printer, 1896-1909.

Steinberg, Arthur. "William Hooper (1742-1790)." John Locke Foundation. *North Carolina History Project*. http://northcarolinahistory.org/encyclopedia/william-hooper-1742-1790/.

Stockton, Richard. "An Expedient for the Settlement of the American Disputes." Reprinted in *The Historical Magazine*, ser. 2, vol. 4 (November 1868): 228-9.

Stout, Neil R. *The Royal Navy in America: 1760-1775*. Annapolis, MD: Naval Institute Press, 1973.

"The Struggle for Independence [Halifax Resolves]." In *North Carolina Manual*. 2008 edition. Raleigh, NC: North Carolina Department of the Secretary of State, 2008.

Suffolk County representatives. "Suffolk Resolves," on September 9, 1774. In Milton Historical Society Archives, box 52. http://www.miltonhistoricalsociety.org/Archives/.

Tanner, Edwin P. *The Province of New Jersey, 1664-1738*. New York: Columbia University, 1908.

Tesón, Fernando R. "Hugo Grotius on War and the State." *Liberty Matters* (essay series). *Liberty Fund*, March 2014, http://oll.libertyfund.org/pages/lm-grotius.

Tindal, Matthew. *Christianity as Old as the Creation*. London, 1730.

Town of Mansfield Official Records. "Mansfield Declaration of Freedom." In *Local History: Mansfield, CT*. http://mansfieldpubliclibraryct.org/history/items/show/294.

Tracy, Nicholas. *Navies, Deterrence, and American Independence: Britain and Seapower in the 1760s and 1770s*. Vancouver: University of British Columbia Press, 1988.

Truman, Harry S. "Address at the National Archives Dedicating the New Shrine for the Declaration of Independence, the Constitution, and the Bill of Rights." *The American Presidency Project*, December 15, 1952. http://www.presidency.ucsb.edu/ws/?pid=14358.

Vereker, Charles. *Eighteenth Century Optimism*. Liverpool, UK: Liverpool University Press, 1967.

Volo, Dorothy Denneen, and Volo, James M. *Daily Life During the American Revolution*. Westport, CT: Greenwood Press, 2003.

The Votes and Proceedings of the Freeholders and other Inhabitants of the Town of Boston. Boston: Edes and Gill, 1772.

Wells, Robert V. *Population of the British Colonies in America Before 1776: A Survey of Census Data*. Princeton, NJ: Princeton University Press, 1975.

"Westmoreland Resolutions." In *Westmoreland County, Virginia: A Short Chapter and Bright Day in its History*. Edited by T. R. B. Wright. Richmond, VA: Whittet & Shepperson, printers, 1912.

Wilding, Norman, and Laundry, Philip. *An Encyclopedia of Parliament.*, 4th ed. London: Cassell and Co., 1972.

William L. Stone. *Life of Joseph Brant-Thayendanegea*. 2 vols. 1838. Reprint, Albany, NY: Munsell, 1865.

Wills, Gary. *Inventing America: Jefferson's Declaration of Independence*. Garden City, NY: Doubleday & Co., 1978.

Wilson, James. "Considerations on the Nature and Extent of the Legislative Authority of the British Parliament." In *Collected Works of James Wilson*. 2 vols. Indianapolis: Liberty Fund, 2007.

Witherspoon, John. "The Dominion of Providence over the Passions of Men." In *Political Sermons of the American Founding Era: 1730-1805*. Volume 1. Indianapolis: Liberty Fund, 1998.

Wolf, Edwin. "The Authorship of the 1774 Address to the King Restudied." *The William and Mary Quarterly* 22, no. 2 (April 1965): 189-224.

Wollaston, William. *The Religion of Nature Delineated.* London, 1722.

Wood, Gordon. *The American Revolution.* New York: Random House, 2002.

INDEX

A
Adams, John 4, 16, 17, 81, 133, 147
Adams, Samuel 12, 30, 50, 52, 56, 147
Aquinas, Thomas 32, 166
arbitrary power 34, 37
Aristotle 28, 106, 115, 165
Articles of Confederation 115

B
Bacon, Francis 8
Barclay, William 33
Bartlett, Josiah 148
Bernard, Francis 13, 53
Bible xii, 27, 66, 124, 164
Blackstone, William 29, 31, 45, 172
Board of Trade 8, 49, 61
Bonaparte, Napoleon 10
Boston Massacre 13
Boston Tea Party 13, 75
Braxton, Carter 159
Burke, Edmund 87

C
calendar (transition) xv
Canada 84
Carroll, Charles (of Carrollton) 126, 145
Charles I 37, 89, 104
charters 22
Chase, Samuel 146
Cicero 31, 165
Clark, Abraham 149
Clymer, George 154
Coercive Acts. See Intolerable Acts
Coke, Edward 38, 168
Commentaries of the Laws of England 172
Committee of Five 20
Common Sense 139
commonwealth 3
consent of the governed 2, 30, 78, 104, 124, 130, 132, 172
Considerations on the Nature and Extent of the Legislative Authority of the British Parliament 132
constitution 165
Continental Association 15, 120
the Creator 23, 27, 111, 118, 164, 166
Cromwell, Oliver 70

D
The Declaration and Resolves of the First Continental Congress 130
Declaration of Independence
  fair copy 18
  process 16, 17, 18, 19, 137
  purpose xiii, xvi, 109
  versions xv
Declaration of the Causes and Necessity of Taking up Arms 110

Index

Declaratory Act 11, 71, 88
Dialogus 167
Dickinson, John 110, 154
Diderot, Denis 9
Discourses Concerning Government 9, 169
divine right of kings 4, 169, 170
Dunlap, John 141

E

Edwards, Jonathan 119
Edward the Confessor 5
Elizabeth I 76
Ellery, William 156
English Bill of Rights 3, 7, 38, 47, 100, 113
Enlightenment xiv, 8, 25, 134, 163
equality 22
executive power 100, 127, 134, 171
Expedient for the Settlement of the American Disputes 129
external taxes 78, 131. See also taxation

F

First Continental Congress 15, 42, 102
Floyd, William 151
Franklin, Benjamin 17, 27, 154
French and Indian War 9, 93

G

Gage, Thomas 9, 11, 53, 68, 72, 92
Gaius 166
Gaspee affair 63, 83, 156
George III 10, 42, 44, 60, 84, 88, 101
Gerry, Elbridge 147
Glorious Revolution 4, 7, 89
government, purpose of 31, 165, 171
Grotius, Hugo 33
Gwinnett, Button 144

H

Hall, Lyman 144
Hancock, John 97, 118, 141, 147
Harrison, Benjamin 159
Hart, John 150
Henry III 6
Hewes, Joseph 130, 152
Heyward, Thomas, Jr. 157
Hoadly, Benjamin 170
Hobbes, Thomas 4, 9, 31, 168
Hooker, Richard 167
Hooper, William 153
Hopkinson, Francis xiii, 135, 150
Hopkins, Stephen 30, 123, 157
Hume, David 171
Huntington, Samuel 142
Hutchinson, Thomas 49, 74, 86

I

Institutes of the Lawes of England 168
internal taxes 78, 131. See also taxation
Intolerable Acts 14, 74

J

James I 6, 38, 120
James II 7, 89, 156
Jefferson, Thomas 17, 42, 110, 159
John I 6
Johnson, Guy 96
judicial power 61, 64, 134, 171
justice 164

L

law of nations 107, 166
Lee, Francis Lightfoot 159
Lee resolution 17, 18, 41, 109, 112
Lee, Richard Henry 17, 41, 112, 120, 159
legislative power 3, 69, 70, 88, 116, 134, 171
the Levellers 37

Leviathan 4, 168
Lewis, Francis 151
liberty, right of 29, 172
life, right of 29, 172
Livingston, Philip 152
Livingston, Robert R. 18, 151
Livy 166
Locke, John 3, 9, 28, 79, 170
Lord Dunmore 98
Lord Hillsborough 53
Lord North 86, 93
Lord Shelburne 73
Lynch, Thomas, Jr. 157

M
Magna Carta 6, 38
Martin, Josiah 51, 152
Mary II 7, 105
Mason, George 26, 81
Massachusetts Circular Letter 12, 52, 147
Matlack, Timothy 19, 161
McKean, Thomas 20, 143
mercantilism 76, 117
mercenaries, foreign 94
Middleton, Arthur 158
Montesquieu 9, 106, 171
Moore, Henry 54, 73
Morris, Lewis 152
Morris, Robert 154
Morton, John 155
Mun, Thomas 117

N
National Archives xii
naturalization 59
natural law 22, 28, 106
natural rights xiii, 26, 28, 104, 130, 167, 170, 172
"The Nature of the Kingdom of Christ" 170
Nelson, Thomas, Jr. 160
Neville, Henry 169

Nicomachean Ethics 106, 165

O
Of The Laws of Ecclesiastical Polity 167
Olive Branch Petition 148
On the Commonwealth 165
Otis, James 13, 37, 56

P
Paca, William 146
Paine, Robert Treat 148
Paine, Thomas 139, 164
Parliament 6, 38, 70, 72, 126
Penn, John 153
people, authority of 2, 22, 100, 111, 116, 169
Petition to the King 42, 137
Philip II of Spain 23
Plato 164
Plato Redivivus 169
Plutarch 166
Politics 165
Prohibitory Act 16, 90, 94
property, right of 29
providence. See the Creator
pursuit of happiness, right of 29, 165, 172

Q
Quartering Act 11

R
Randolph, Edmund 113
Read, George 144
reason 28
rebellion, right of 32
redress of grievances 8, 104
representation in Parliament 79, 124, 133
The Republic 164
Revolutionary War 15, 91
Richard II 55

Index

The Rights of Colonies Examined 124, 157
Rodney, Caesar 144
Rogers, John 145
Ross, George 155
Rousseau, Jean-Jacques 171
royal charter 6, 69, 104, 116, 156
royal disallowance 47
Rush, Benjamin 155
Rutledge, Edward 158

S

Second Continental Congress xiii, 2, 15, 110, 123
Second Treatise of Government 3, 9, 28, 170
Seven Years' War. See French and Indian War
Sharpe, Horatio 55
Sherman, Roger 18, 142
Sidney, Algernon xiv, 9, 169
Six Nations 96
slavery 98, 157
Smith, Adam 9, 76, 172
Smith, James 155
social contract 168
The Social Contract 171
The Spirit of the Laws 9, 171
Stamp Act 10, 67, 101, 120, 124, 168
standing army 66, 131
state of nature 34, 169
Stockton, Richard 128, 150
Stone, Thomas 146
Sugar Act 10, 65
A Summary View of the Rights of British America 42, 88
Summa Theologica 166

T

Tacitus 166
taxation 78, 124, 131
Taylor, George 155
Thompson, Charles 141

Thomson, Charles 160
Thornton, Matthew 149
Thoughts on Government 134
Townshend Acts 12, 52, 54, 62, 65, 73
A Treatise of Human Nature 171
Treaty of Paris 67
Treaty of Union 71
Tresilian, Robert 55
trial by jury 8, 80, 104
Truman, Harry S. xii
Tyron, William 51

V

von Pufendorf, Samuel 169

W

Walton, George 144
Warren, Joseph 56, 103
Washington, George 9, 67
The Wealth of Nations 9, 172
Westmoreland Resolutions 120
Whipple, William 149
William II of Normandy 5
William III 7, 8, 105
William of Ockham 167
Williams, William 143
Wilson, James 131, 156
Witherspoon, John 118, 150
Wolcott, Oliver 143
Wollaston, William 29
Wythe, George 160

About the Author

Tim Patrick is an author, software architect, and lover of history. He has published nearly a dozen books, mostly on technology topics, and is a regular magazine contributor. As the founder and host of the *Well-Read Man Project* (wellreadman.com), he offers regular commentary on current events, politics, history, and books old and new.

For more than three decades, Tim has spent each day developing custom software applications for small- and medium-sized businesses. Way back in 2007, Microsoft welcomed Tim into its Most Valuable Professional (MVP) program thanks to the assistance he provides to beginning and intermediate developers. He earned his computer science degree from Seattle Pacific University, and began work on his very first book while sitting in a class at that prestigious institution.

About the Series

In a world awash in nearly unlimited information, the *Understand in One Afternoon* series helps you discover the essentials of important subjects in a reasonable amount of time. Each book is designed to be consumed in about four hours—in one afternoon—and offers a core grounding in topics ranging from current events to technology, from philosophy to business.

www.ingramcontent.com/pod-product-compliance
Lightning Source LLC
Chambersburg PA
CBHW070620100426
42744CB00006B/553